T0365534

RUNT TO WARRIOR

INFANTRY COMPANY SCOUT, LEAD MAN, "POINT"

IRVIN L. BORING

Order this book online at www.trafford.com
or email orders@trafford.com

Most Trafford titles are also available at major online book retailers.

© Copyright 2009 Irvin Boring.
All rights reserved. No part of this publication may be reproduced, stored
in a retrieval system, or transmitted, in any form or by any means, electronic,
mechanical, photocopying, recording, or otherwise, without
the written prior permission of the author.

Note for Librarians: A cataloguing record for this book is available from Library
and Archives Canada at www.collectionscanada.ca/amicus/index-e.html

Printed in Victoria, BC, Canada.

ISBN: 978-1-4251-5612-1 (soft)
ISBN: 978-1-4251-5613-8 (ebook)

*Our mission is to efficiently provide the world's finest, most
comprehensive book publishing service, enabling every author to
experience success. To find out how to publish your book, your way, and
have it available worldwide, visit us online at www.trafford.com*

Trafford rev. 10/19/2009

 www.trafford.com

North America & international
toll-free: 1 888 232 4444 (USA & Canada)
phone: 250 383 6864 ♦ fax: 812 355 4082

SITUATIONS

1. It is predawn on a morning of a day in March 1945; the temperature is near freezing and I am without winter garments. Lying in a pipe, on my stomach with my legs straight and my arms extended above my head I have no room to roll from side to side. I dare not move a muscle for fear of being detected; all the while I am praying to my god that no dogs are present in the area to give away my being there.

While laying there I think, "Whose fault is it that you are in such a predicament? Not poorly educated mom and dad who struggled from the day they were married, to raise a family while living in perpetual poverty. You idiot; you have no one to blame but yourself. Think, and think, and think; turn back the years, do anything to keep the mind alert." The hours drag by. I am so cold and stiff I think I will surely die. Attempting to get out of this situation after about six hours have elapsed, my body fails to respond.

2. I cannot get my breath; I have to get out of this room and get some tobacco smoke into my lungs.

3. The night is clear and as I stand in the tree line making my observation of the field before me; the moonlight

affords me enough light to make out a heap on the ground about thirty feet from my position. I cannot believe my childhood habit of coming across dead bodies has kicked in.

4. I rub my eyes to make sure I am not hallucinating, for what I see through the dim light of darkness before me, is a scene one would expect to see in a weird nightmare or movie.

5. "Lieutenant: If you ever do that to me again I'll shoot your ass."

6. "Look: His brains are hanging out."

7. People with good hearing had better insert earplugs.

DEDICATION

This book is dedicated to the memory of my parents, "MARY ELIZABETH RAGER BORING and JOSEPH HALE BORING," who put so much time, so much effort and so much love into the struggle of rearing a spindly chronically ill child; "me," draining the love away from my siblings.

I also dedicate it in honor and memory of all my predecessors, who held one or the other, or even both of the two positions of "INFANTRY COMPANY SCOUT" and the "LEAD MAN," also known as "POINT."

Contents

ξ GROWING YEARS ξ

ξ TRAINING FOR WAR ξ

ξ COMBAT ξ

AUTHOR'S NOTES

This story is written with the intent of paying homage to, "the Infantry Company Scouts," who were lone operatives behind the enemy lines. Most of my scout predecessors did not return from their final mission and the only accolades they received were a posthumous, "Purple Heart Medal," issued to their next of kin.

They gave their lives while on patrol or reconnaissance only to be one of a forgotten lot. There was no one to tell their story so I am striving to put as much insight as possible into what they endured.

It is also to pay homage to the "Lead Man" also known as "Point," who is several hundred yards out in front of, and leading the way for the main body of troops.

I wish there was some way for a second or third party to tell this story because it sounds so full of arrogance and self grandeur on my part. That is not the intent, but, I was there and walked in their shoes, or, "footsteps," so I use my first hand experience only to demonstrate what it took, "To be one of them."

Many men of my platoon died but I cannot remember their proper names. You ask the question, "What is the reason for such a weak memory that you cannot remember the names of the men who were so close?" That same misgiving occurred to me, until I talked with other combat veterans. We discussed the issue of our buddies in combat and how strange that we were so close, and were willing to die for one another, but we cannot recall their proper names. Of course if you trained for war as a unit you were familiar with your long time buddies, but if you were thrown into combat as a replacement, you were, "A Greenhorn," so the combat hardened troops kept you under close scrutiny until you proved you had the right stuff. I was of the latter and operated more or less as a loner, so you will see why names are not embedded in my memory. Retention of names was difficult for me because I seldom fought among the mass.

I am humbled to associate myself with men of such courage. I feel I have the great need, (NOT TO TOUT MY OWN IMPORTANCE), but to use my own childhood experiences to illustrate that my predecessor's childhoods surely must have been similar to mine.

In a number of events I stress the fact that many nameless soldiers displayed a greater degree of courage than myself. The saying is,"War is stranger than fiction:" If you do not believe this fact, stop reading right here. You must also keep in mind that through it all I held the lowly rank of Private First Class.

Since my stay with Infantry Company "B" was so brief, I more or less depict myself as, "A stranger who passed and left footprints." The experiences I endured during my growing years prepared me to deal with almost every situation I encountered in combat.

This is in no way an authenticated chronicle of the war, the events are not documented by war records, and the events are simply in as accurate a sequence as possible. Nothing in these writings is endorsed or sanctioned, by anyone other than the author and everything is simply as I remember them.

To my knowledge I am the only private in the United States Army to be addressed as, "Mister" (except for roll calls, of course). I was addressed as, "Mister Lee" by my fellow enlisted men, my overseeing Non Commissioned Officers, as well as by my Superior Officers.

A great portion of this story is not pleasant reading, but in order to keep it a true story, and for clarity, events must include all the ugly details, as well the good.

FORWARD

For fifty six years after WWII ended in Europe on May 7, 1945, I stayed silent and kept the war bottled up inside my head; not relating any of my war experiences to a living soul. I kept my family awake with my screams and shenanigans, and I had not one peaceful night's sleep in all these years, as I relived those terrible experiences in the form of night mares.

I believed I was too much of a man to seek consoling. In 1999 I had a year long, near death episode that confined me to bed most of the time, so I lay there doing a lot of soul searching. Defying all odds I recuperated and got back on my feet and at the first possible opportunity I visited a library and discovered there was a veteran's association of my wartime outfit.

In November of 2000 I joined "The Yankee Division Veterans Association" and with encouragement from my comrades I related a few of my experiences, and discovered several revelations. I had made a terrible error by staying silent; bringing it out in the open gave me great peace of mind, and since then I have not had a single nightmare.

Another terrible mistake on my part was in not writing eulogies to the loved ones of the men who died while in the act of protecting me. I know this sounds ludicrous, but for several years I have contacted all known war archives and sources of possible information, for proof that I was ever in combat, and to acquire names of these men. All my efforts have been in vain.

There are those who would dispute several of my narrations, for they are depicted in a manner unbecoming The United States Military. For this reason I use only titles instead of names, except for a few occasions. I have already stated the other reason why I do not use names.

୧ **GROWING YEARS** ୧

CHAPTER

1

FIRST EIGHTEEN MONTHS

My first breath is taken on June 30, 1926, in the last house on the southwest side of Hemlock Street, (a dirt road) located just outside of Morrellville, a suburb of Johnstown, Pennsylvania. I have no recollection of the first few month of my life, but do have memories from that time on.

The front porch of the house extends across the entire width of the front of the house and is separated by about a ten foot bank, sloping from the base of the house down to the street. As soon as I am old enough my brother Carl, who was two years and one week old the day I was born, carries me, or I crawl to the front porch, where the two of us look between the pickets of the porch railing and watch buggies, carriages, wagons and people slowly pass by on the street, traveling from our left to our right.

The thing that stands out most to me in any of these processions, is a wagon with its seat occupied by a driver and his assistant, while the rest of the space on the wagon is overflowing with beautiful flowers. Carl explains to me, "The wagon is carrying the coffin with a dead person in it who is going to be buried in the cemetery." It is not long after I start watching these processions until a beautiful black truck sometimes appears in the procession in place of the flower wagon. The procession comes to a halt until someone removes the two cross poles from a gate, then the procession proceeds through the gate, either going straight, or it turns right, inside the gate.

My first observations of these processions is done in beautiful warm weather, but it is not long until Carl and I have to bundle up in heavy clothing to watch these processions from the porch and I see my first snow flakes on Thanksgiving day. As I progress to the age of awareness, and start walking and improve my walking skills, I start spending time in the back yard and I notice a wagon path separating two sides of the yard from a split log fence. Carl explains to me, "The fence and all the head stones beyond is a cemetery, where people go when they die."

As I walk along the side of the house next to the cemetery I see the main entrance to the cemetery, to the immediate right, is separated from the porch by about ten feet of yard and the alley. I observe the funeral processions as they pass through the cemetery gate, immediately turn right, and the horse proceeds to pull the wagon up a wagon path making me wonder, "How can a lone horse climb such a steep path pulling a wagon, loaded with two people, with a coffin and with all the floral arrangements?" Later in the day I see people on foot, people riding horses and small rigs come back down the path and exit the cemetery, but the wagon that carried the coffin and all the floral arrangements never does, so I wonder, "What happened to the wagon?"

I also notice a very small building in the yard that is being visited by all the people I know. Upon entering it I detect this foul odor, it is the outhouse and when I am potty trained it is Carl's job to lift me onto the seat, hold me to keep me from falling through the hole, and then he has to wipe my butt.

Carl and I crawl through the cemetery split log fence and explore the cemetery. As our excursions take us farther and farther into the cemetery, I become aware it is "L," shaped with not one noticeable flat spot to be found in its entirety. The one exception is the road inside the gate that separates the cemetery into two sections. Carl was born smart; I believe he could read the first day he laid eyes on a word, and I keep getting astray of him, because all he wants to do is read the epitaph and name written on each of the head stones.

As we venture farther and farther from the house, we eventually reach the upper most part of the cemetery and my question, "What happened to the floral wagon," is answered. The path terminates at a gate that allows in and out traffic to Mountain Road.

Venturing farther to the right in the cemetery we come to a foot path that starts at the top of a steep bank on the upper side of Hemlock Street. Only the stout at heart can make the climb. Another way to get to the cemetery entrance to this path is by taking the alley next to our house. This foot path is very steep and ties in with the wagon path at the gate to Mountain Road. I am very sickly, but when I am up to it, the first eighteen months of my life are spent exploring the cemetery, and the forest above Mountain Road.

I do not remember any of the beginning of my eating frenzy, but as soon as I am old enough to understand that I have an unusual craving for food, I am told mom could not supply enough milk for me. To compensate for this I am fed very soft ground up food along with Mom's milk. Because of my enormous appetite, I am weaned much sooner than most infants and I cry constantly from hunger. Shortly after I am weaned from breast feeding and am consuming solid food I become so frail I am a skeleton with skin stretched over it, Mom feeds me everything imaginable, with the hope of putting some weight on me. I have a ravenous appetite and because I never leave the table until all the food is gone, at a very young age I am nicknamed, "Cleanup." My craving for food creates a big problem and makes it very difficult for Mom because Dad does not earn enough money to buy the necessary amount of food to feed his family. On the other hand, we are without refrigeration of any type, so cooked food can be kept only a few hours. Mom is happy to see me consume everything but the bones of the food left on anyone's plate.

So much food slides down my throat that my stomach bulges. It isn't long after the table is cleared until I am crying and Mom asks my brother Carl, "What's Lee crying about?"

"He's hungry," Carl replies:

Mom exclaim; "He can't be; we just ate."

Because food cannot be kept and I have not left any on the table, there is nothing to snack on but Mom's home made bread. She has Carl cut me a slice off of a round loaf and as I soon as I see him spreading the slice of bread with butter I quit crying.

While the rest of the family eat their eggs cooked for breakfast, because of my anemia, I break as many as six raw eggs onto my plate, add lots of salt and pepper, whip them with a fork, then sop this slimy concoction up with thick slices of Mom's home made bread, spread thick with butter.

The phrase, "spread with butter," is a misnomer. As I get old enough to help Mom, I find out what we call butter is nothing but lard we color with yellow food coloring stirred into it to make it look like butter. I love the mixing of the lard and coloring, using my freshly washed hands to do the mixing. It is a great feeling to have the greasy lard squeeze through my fingers, as I clench and unclench my fists.

CHAPTER
2

OUR HOUSE

The month of January 1928, I am eighteen months old and our family of four is living free gratis in the house owned by Aunt Goldie who's family also consists of four people. Mom is again pregnant with child, and the house is not large enough to accommodate another person, so with their meager money, Mom and Dad, find a very cheap piece of property down one imaginary street from the house in which we live and purchase it. It is the very upper beginning of a gully, (a useless piece of property), that no one wants, so Dad (we never speak of him as Father) acquires it for just a few dollars.

This date January 1928, is the start of a new phase in my life. The gully is nothing more than a deep depression in the ground, so before dad can start building a house in it, the ground level has to be raised. The drop off into the gully (looking up hill) is a distance of about a hundred feet from the left edge of Ash Road. Carl is three and a half, and I am eighteen months old. Dad works twelve hours a day six days a week, so Carl and I curtail our explorations of the cemetery and the forest above it to contribute to the task.

Dad shows Carl and me what needs to be done, of which the first thing is to create an access from Ash Road over to the gully. What can a three and a half and an eighteen month old accomplish? Carl is big enough to awkwardly manipulate a pick and shovel so he fills mine and his little buckets with dirt (mostly top soil) and we carry them to the gully and dump the dirt into it. We do not make much of a dent in the leveling of the area, but every little bit helps, and Dad gives us false praise for what we accomplish. With all the food I consume I should be getting fat, instead I keep getting skinnier and weaker, until Dad takes me to see our doctor, who diagnoses me as extremely anemic and he tells Mom, "Keep stuffing your son with rich food."

Dad, working in his spare time, gets the fill to where he can start building his house; and what a spacious house he starts and creates. He goes into the forest, above the cemetery and fells six good straight trees, about twelve inches in diameter. Using a borrowed horse and wagon he hauls them to the area above the gully, cuts them to his desired length, and assists Carl and me in stripping them of their bark. He applies a heavy coat of creosote to prevent the wood from rotting and being eaten by termites. He then places them in the ground.

He builds two rooms on these six posts, then tops these rooms with a flat roof covered with tarpaper. For reasons unbeknownst to me, instead of placing the entrance door to the house on the uphill side of the house, (where you could just walk right in without steps), Dad places the entrance on the downhill side, with fifteen steps, no hand rails, and no landing at the top. We now have our house that is situated at the head of the gully. Transferring our belongings is a slow process, so we move in during the last week in June, and in a couple of days I will be two years old. June 30 comes and goes with no mention of my birthday because Mom is so heavy with child she can hardly get around.

Seven days later on July 7, 1928, Mom is screaming with so much pain, Carl and I think she is dying. Carl is sent to the old house to have Aunt Goldie come to the house to take care of mom. When Aunt Goldie arrives Carl and I are sent out to play until we are called to come back in. We do not play; we fidget with worry, as we listen to Mom' screams. After a while the screaming stops and in a short period of time, we hear cries of a baby and we are called in to meet our new baby brother, Richard Jay.

It is a miracle; Mom, who was screaming from pain, just a few minutes ago, now has a smile and a serene look on her face. One or the other of my aunts, comes by a couple of times a day, for several days to service the baby, and see that we have cooked food, a bath and clean clothes until Mom is back on her feet. Five of us are now living in a two room house.

CHAPTER
3

ANEMIA AND DIET

Mom and Dad are desperate in their attempts at putting weight on me. I am so frail, and as the days go by I keep losing weight that I cannot afford to lose. I am about three, when my uncle comes by once a day with his beer delivery wagon and supplies me with a glass of beer. The shell of a raw egg is cracked and its contents are dropped into the glass. I am forced to drink the beer containing the unbroken egg yoke, and me being so small, the yoke is a mouth full. I hold my breath and make a number of attempts at swallowing before I finally maneuver the yoke to the point where it breaks and goes down my throat.

You will not hear more laughter at the circus than I hear from all the spectators. This goes on for several years. It is the spectacle of the day and watching me drink it makes my uncle's trip worthwhile.

In the market the butcher grinds a portion of fresh ham, along with beef; thus the word hamburger. Mom mixes this hamburger in a bowl with all the ingredients for meat loaf. When the mixing is completed, she watches me dip my fingers into the bowl, eat until cannot hold any more, and this sustains me until meal time. I am fed this raw meat, but for the rest of the family's eating, it is baked and served as meatloaf, or it is fried for hamburgers. My brothers cannot watch as I eat this concoction of raw meat, or the gooey mess of raw eggs.

Instead of gaining any weight I now start losing pounds that I cannot afford to lose and I am becoming so weak I am having trouble walking. My left leg is degenerating and has red patches, (no - not red, but discolored splotches under the skin, so in their desperation Mom and Dad take me to our family doctor, who has me hospitalized. After a never ending series of tests I hear Mom and Dad being told, "Mister and Misses Boring, please sit down because I have devastating news to tell you. All tests indicate your son has leukemia in his left leg bone." The words having no meaning to me.

I do not know what treatment I am receiving, but each week I put on a little weight and the red spots under my skin disappear. Each X-ray shows a reduction in the size of the spots in my bone marrow and I regain my strength. Upon being discharged from my hospital stay of three month Mom and Dad are instructed to have my leg X-rayed every six month. Back at home I learn to walk all over again and before long I resume my old habits and activities. Misdiagnosis: Not so: (see post war, war connections).

I am about three years old and start making lone excursions into the forest. I am fascinated at all the edibles that grow there. I do not spend much time playing; most of my time is spent in the forest foraging for all varieties of these delicious kinds of edibles. I learn to walk with a cautious step, because tiny delicate plants grow among the fallen dead leaves, and these would never be seen by the average person, but with my ravenous appetite I am not average. Locating traces of these delicate plants,I kneel down, move the leaves, and find different flavored berries. My favorite having the taste of Spearmint. There is an inconspicuous green plant, about six inches tall I call May apples' and has no trace of any kind of fruit, but moving aside the leaves, I expose a light green fruit, about ¾ of an inch in diameter that has a nice sweet taste as I chew it.

My excursions take me farther and farther into the woods, and I spent hour after hour, eating the delicacies I come across. There are crab apples, that are small size for an apple, but chewing the hard sour apple in its entirety is worth the effort. The large wild grapevines that hang down from the tree limbs are loaded with small grapes, which are of not much significance to me, but the new shoots of the vine are just the opposite, because I really enjoy breaking them off and chewing them for the moist, sour juice. Some areas have scattered patches of blackberry vines, with berries as large as my thumb while other areas are dense with huckleberry bushes, thickly laden with berries that I eat hand full after hand full.

As I walk under certain trees the soles of my bare feet become purple from squishing the tiny cherries that cover the ground. They are about the size of a large pea, and consist of a seed with a thin purple skin. We call these cherries, chokecherries, and they only drop to the ground when they are overly ripe or rotten, so I climb the tree, crawl out on the branches to where I can reach the cherries. Sitting there I pick the cherries, pop them into my mouth one at a time, suck the skin off the seed and spitting out the seed, I consume dozen after dozen of these cherries and I do not get my stomach full but I do end up with an awful purple face around my mouth area. After eating these cherries until I am hungry, I go home and eat a good hearty meal. Mom's main dish is home grown, chucked peas, and fresh potatoes boiled together. This may not seem appetizing, but it is food and it eases my hunger.

An abundance and variety of nut trees grow in the forest, with some of tree trunks being as large as two feet in diameter. I find most of the nuts that drop to the ground are defective, so at first I tuck my sack under my belt and climb the trees with small trunks, and I am able to pick as many nuts as needed. Nuts are a big staple around holiday times, so my tree climbing ability enables me to keep Mom supplied with all the nuts she needs for baking and salads. As I improve my tree climbing skill, I take on larger trees, and eventually I decide it is time, to climb this monstrous one growing on the edge of a knoll. My arms only reach about halfway around it, but the bark is rough enough for me to get finger and toe holds, (I do not wear shoes.) Being just skin and bones, I have no weight to speak of, so I climb the tree, and have to work my way out on the limbs as far as I can to get to where the nuts are growing. This act sometimes finds me on a limb out over the ravine. It is scary with all that space below me, but fear is not a factor when food is involved. When I have a sufficient amount of nuts in the sack, I take the length of string out of my pocket, tie the sack shut and drop it to the ground. Arriving home with my sack full of a variety of nuts, the entire family spends hour after hour cracking nuts and extracting the nut meat.

Being a very sickly child from the time I make a live appearance into Mom and Dad"s world, it takes all their time and efforts to keep me alive, so I am afraid their efforts to do so deprives my siblings of a lot of parental love. It is not long after my bout with leukemia until I develop a chronic earache in my left ear. When my constant crying gets on Dad's nerves he sits me on his knee, with my left side to him and blows warm cigarette smoke into my ear. This relieves the pain for an hour or two, then it is the same scenario all over again.

It is not longer than six months after we move into our two room house, before Dad starts the first enlargement of the house. He removes a section of the dividing wall, behind the stove between the two rooms, builds a brick chimney, starting at the floor, up through the roof, extending to a ridiculous heights, up in the air. He reroutes the stove pipe into the chimney, and covers the old hole in the roof.

He constructs a very steep roof to prevent the snow from accumulating on it during the winter, thus creating an attic. The top of the chimney sticks up about three feet above the peak of the roof and now looks normal. At the right end of the attic, over the bedroom, he installs louvers, and on the left over the kitchen he installs a small louvered door to afford access to the attic. He builds and secures a wooden ladder from the ground up the outside wall of the kitchen to this door. Enough area of the floor joists centered under the peak of the roof and above the kitchen is covered with boards, making walking around room for Carl and me. Carl and I now have our own bedroom, so the bedding from our bed is raised to the attic by use of a rope and the blankets are spread on the floor, then our pillows are placed on them close to the chimney.

After being cautioned, to be very careful never to upset the kerosene lamp; we place it in the basket we have tied on the end of the raising rope and raise it to the attic where it is placed on the floor at arms length from our sleeping blankets. We sleep with our heads, next to the chimney, with the perpetual heat from the warm bricks providing welcome heat during the winter, and keeping us sweltering during the summer.

You would think the two of us boys sleeping in the attic would afford some privacy for Mom and Dad; not so, for I awake during the night with my terrible left earache, move cautiously to the door, climb down the ladder and barge in on them seeking relief. Dad gets up, gives me his smoke treatment that soothes the pain and we all go back to our beds and sleep until the next ache.

Every hour of my days are consumed with necessary tasks and with me being all energy, I still find time to participate in all my favorite activities. At the end of my day when I climb the ladder and collapse on my blankets, the muscles in my body are so tense and taut that poor Carl does not get his proper sleep because the relaxing of my muscles causes me to twitch and jerk all over our bedding.

I develop a nasty, constant cough and so much phlegm builds up in my throat that it is extremely difficult for me to breath. Anyone escorting me anywhere, spends a lot of time standing in back of me, with their arms around my waist, holding me as I go though a coughing spell and up chuck this phlegm. When I am finished, I am so exhausted I lay on the ground until I get back my strength and composure. Dad-and this sounds disgusting- often reaches into my mouth with his fingers and pulls out long strings of phlegm that look like wads of yarn, giving me temporary relief.

After all the known home remedies fail to cure my cough I am taken to see our family doctor who explains to my parents, "All that coughing and the build up of phlegm in Lee's throat is due to his having chronic bronchitis. There is not much that can be done about it, so I suggest having him smoke Cool Menthol cigarettes." When I am strangling from the air passages being clogged, a couple of puffs from a cigarette causes me to throw up, expelling a large amount of the phlegm.

My two brothers and I come down with the mumps and the measles at the same time. Mom and Dad set up the old kid's bed in the kitchen where they sleep and put the three of us in their bed by the window. We are not allowed out of it except to use the slop jar. Light is not good for the measles, so a heavy blanket is hung across the windows to make the bedroom as dark as possible. Can you possibly visualize what Mom goes through in taking care of us, not to mention keeping the three of us from each others throats?

Besides taking care of us, Mom has to perform all the chores that are assigned to Carl and me. Due to the run down condition of my body, my measles are so severe the others are up and about long before me. Somehow we all survive this ordeal and we all go back to our regular sleeping arrangements.

It is not long after we get over the measles until the three of us brothers are going through the same scenario; this time it is the chickenpox. After all the scabs fall off and time passes none of us are left with any physical pox marks.

We raise two or three pigs for our own consumption and I am assigned the responsibility of every phase of taking care of them. I help Dad build the pigpens, make repairs and clean the pens as needed. I am also charged with keeping the pigs well fed. Dumping the slop down the shoot into the feeding trough is called, "slopping the hogs."

The burlap sack I carry into the forest for gathering acorns is about twice the size of my body. The forest above the cemetery is sparsley populated with large oak trees, so filling the sack with fallen acorns is very easy. These fallen acorns range in size from very small to as large as a young boy's thumb.

I quickly learn to distinguish the new freshly fallen acorns from ones that fell the previous year. The time consuming part of filling the sack is so many acorns in the sack, then after taking time to cut and peel one with my pocket knife it ends up in my stomach etc, etc. When the sack is as full of acorns as I can manage, I drag it to the hog pen and dump the hog's share into the trough.

Since the only refrigeration is ice chests, the dairy's delivery wagons and stores can only keep dairy products for one day, so the dairy delivery man takes all the day old items back to the dairy, where they have a room constructed of cement walls and floor with a drain in the middle of the floor. The returned milk is dumped down this drain.

It is the dairy's policy that rather than waste all this perfectly good milk, anyone who wants it can take all the milk they want if they are at the dairy before the dumping. I have buckets with lids that I place in my home made wagon and pull the two miles to the dairy located in Johnstown, timing my arrival to be there before the delivery wagons arrive. If I am there before they dump I am allowed all I want for free, but they will not save any for me.

Milk is churned to make butter and the byproduct of this churning is buttermilk that is then sold, but there is not much demand for it. Huge amounts of it is returned and dumped down the drain. Milk is not homogenized and I love the taste of the whole milk; there is no better taste to me than when I fill my mouth, swish it around and slowly let it go down my throat. Each trip I drink until my stomach is full, because I really have a taste for all the different kinds of milk. When my stomach will hold no more I fill the buckets and make the long trek home. The buckets are filled with perfectly good milk, and Mom has made sure the buckets have all been thoroughly cleaned before I made my trip. Retracing my route through Cambria City and Morrellville, I arrive home. The milk is either warm or cold depending on the temperature of the day, and the entire family has no qualms about consuming their share.

The pigs are my responsibility from start to finish. I travel the neighborhood pulling my little red wagon collecting edible garbage from the housewives. Dad manages to buy large sacks of some kind of a brown mash, so after I have a last drink of the milk I hauled home from the dairy I mix the remainder with the mash and garbage I have accumulated.

When I dump this repulsive mixture into the chute of the trough, I enjoy listening to the pigs snorting and blowing bubbles in their food when they are eating from their slop trough. I do not understand how they keep from strangling, since they never lift their snouts out of the trough. The pigs are, pun intended, "In hog heaven."

I am always being asked, "Did you get any slop today, did you mix the slop," and, "did you slop the hogs?" This repulsive mixture keeps the hogs growing nicely until just before butchering time, then I feed them all the ears of corn they can consume until they are nice and fat. I keep the pigs in their hog heaven, but I never make a pet of any of them because to me they are just "garbage disposals and good sausage."

The great depression is in progress. As difficult and as hard as it was for Dad to earn money to feed his family in normal times, it is now next to impossible to keep food on the table unless we grow your own food. Dad is an extremely hard worker and in gratitude to the man who took him, "Joe," under his guidance as a nine year old and paid him just a minimal wage as an apprentice carpenter would never quit the man and is still working for practically the same meager wage. The construction of new homes and the repair of existing home has come to a standstill so Dad's income is $0. The neighbors respect Dad and know his plight so the ones who can afford to part with food, bring peck bags of staple foods to our door.

Besides bringing home all the various nuts from the forest, I also do my part in contributing my share of food to the family larder by scouring the neighborhood of it's dandelion plants. Returning home and presenting Mom with my two large flour bags filled with the plants, is like manna from heaven to Mom, because now we will have a nice green, wilted salad set on the supper table. In my efforts to fill my bags, I sometimes extend my search approximately a mile from the house, ending at the Westmont airport. Each side of the runway has acre after acre of grass with a density of the dandelion plants, so I never fail to fill the two bags. In our desperation for greens I rid the yard of it's wide bladed grass and any leafy plants I can find. These make a fine tasting wilted salad. No, this grass eating does not create milk in our bodies.

As soon as my body becomes tall and strong enough to wield a shovel and garden tools, I till the soil in any plot of ground that I find lying vacant around our neighborhood. On school days Mom, who is last to bed, first to rise, rouses me out of bed just before first light, and when I am dressed, I carry the tools to any one of these chosen plots. When I start this spading routine I am really not large enough to maneuver the shovel properly but I persevere and eventually grow into the task.

When I am notified by one of my brothers that breakfast is ready I return to the house. I remove my shoes, (shoes are a necessity for spading with the pointed shovel), I eat and then I go to school. Returning home from school, I go through the gardening routine. I eat my supper, I return to the plot, I prepare the spaded soil for planting, and when it gets too dark to see I go home and go to bed. On days there is no school I am at one or the other of the garden plots from first light until dusk, tilling the soil and planting many types of seeds with many of them being planted in corn.

Mom removes the galvanized tub from its peg on the kitchen wall, places the tub on the kitchen table and pours a lot of flour and water into it. She then dissolves baker's yeast in a pan of hot water, lets it sit until it cools down, then pours it into the tub and starts mixing with her hands. I sit right up on the kitchen table and watch as she mixes, adds more water, on and on until the front of her is all white and the dough is the desired consistency. She then spreads a large white cloth over the dough, places the tub on the metal shelf on the back of the kitchen's wood burning stove, and lets it sit over night to allow the heat from the stove to make the dough rise into a huge mound. In the morning she takes it down from the shelf, places it on the table and using her fisted hands, kneads the dough until it is back down to normal. She then breaks off chunks. These chunks are formed into a ball and placed into round metal baking pans. These pans are placed into the oven, four at a time, and baked until the bread is a nice golden brown.

When the loaves are removed from the oven and cooled enough to handle, one of the loaves makes the ultimate sacrifice. The aroma of baking bread has everyone in a frenzy, and we just cannot wait any longer for a crust of nice warm bread. Everyone has to have a crust, so Mom slices off pieces, all around the loaf until the crust is exhausted. We then spread a liberal amount of our so called butter on them, and eat. Now the remainder of the loaf is mutilated and consumed. What a treat!

I am nine years old, in third grade and I have pretty well beaten the bronchitis, so I no longer smoke and it is such a relief to cough only occasionally. My tonsils become infected and I go to the hospital to have them removed. Of course I cannot go home a couple of days after the surgeon has removed them like everyone else does. Instead I remain in the hospital several months.

Being home from my tonsil operation only a few weeks, I start to shake. I develop a severe jerk and twitch. I lose all my equilibrium so severely that I can not stand or walk. Back in the hospital once again, I am intensely cold and shiver so much that I am covered with, (hold on to your hat) thirteen layers of blankets. I still cannot stop shivering. After a series of tests the doctor tells Mom and Dad, "Tests confirm Lee has St. Vitas's Dance."

Blood is extracted from my arms every thirty minutes. On the hour it is taken from the inside crook of my left elbow, and on the half hour it is taken from the inside crook of my right elbow. The needles are shaped like fountain pen points and make an incision each time blood is taken.

There is no shame in all of my crying because I am one scared little boy. The inside of my both elbows are mounded with scar tissue build up. Dad weighs one hundred and fifty pounds and on one occasion he is holding my left hand down, keeping my arm straight for the doctor to extract blood from my left arm. The pain of the needle is so intense that I lift Dad off the floor. I do not know what medications I am given, but after three months I hear the doctor inform Mom and Dad, "I've done all I can, so take him home and have him learn to live with any after symptoms that may occur." I am released from the hospital and when back at home I refuse to give up. With my determination to get well and be equal to the other boys I beat all the odds and in six months I am completely normal. Missing most of the school year, I am forced to repeat the third grade.

CHAPTER
4

VILE NASTY THINGS

For about the first three years of my life I am so shy, I cannot talk to people older than myself. On Halloween, young adults dressed as clowns, hobos, etc, come to the door, trick or treating; not for the treats, but for the plain fun of it. When the door is opened the sight of them scares me to such an extreme that I tremble, I scream, and I cry. Mom tries to restrain me at the door, but I will have none of it; I run to my bed and hide under it until all the scary people leave.

I can not learn anything academic, such as reading and spelling. Dad understands that, like him, I will never be an intellectual. He directs my education along another path. He recognizes my potentials lay in the direction of common sense and mechanical understanding, so he guides my education towards the hard, harsh realities of life. He has me perform all kinds of demeaning and heart rendering acts that no child should be exposed too. In doing so he shapes my life to where my shyness disappears and I can overcome any and all diversities.

I never have a thought of rebelling against my parents for making me do these things because I idolize them and know in my small mind that the things have to be done. Little does Dad realize how much he is training me to be a man among men and also training me for war. He prepares me to overcome fear and shows me how to get the task done. I do not hate him for making me do these distasteful things, but I sure do hate doing the vile things he demands of me.

Our pet cat has a litter of kittens, so before Dad leaves for work in the morning he gives me the order, "Put the whole litter into a sack, take it to the pond. When I come home from work I want them gone." It is the same with the grown cats when they get sick. So, crying all the while, I put the victims in a burlap sack, carry the sack to the pond, place it into the water and submerge and hold the whole thing under until all struggling ceases. Then the kittens or the cat get their funeral. I shed many a tear as this happens time after time.

When our pet dogs become afflicted with distemper, we can not afford a veterinarian, so we break open 22 caliber shells, remove the gun powder and mix it into the dog food as a medication. Of course this does not work, so as the affliction worsens and the dog can not be cured; Dad orders me, "Lee; take (whatever name they have) into the woods, and when I come home tonight I want it gone."

I tie a rope around my pet's neck, take my 22 rifle, as well as a shovel and lead it into the forest above the cemetery where I tie it to a tree. While crying; I look him or her in the eye over the rifle sight, take a couple of gulps to get myself under control and pull the trigger. As I look a pet dog in the eye, before pulling the trigger it seems him or her are telling me; "It is all right Lee; I understand." I then dig a little grave and give the carcass a proper burial, all the while having tears run down my cheeks.

With my large pointed nose, my recessed chin, my over lapping bottom front teeth, no flesh on my bones, and the eye patch I wear over my right eye, because my left eye is known as weak eye, I am very conscious of my looks and I hate it. I am so self conscious of my looks "ugliness" and inability to learn anything, that it is terrible on me.

A neighbor lady is taking pity on such a frail little seven year old and is preparing me fried, canned tuna fish. The aroma given off from the hot skillet is wonderful and of course I am ravished. We are sitting at her kitchen table eating the delicious tasting fish that is a new taste to me, (because my parents cannot afford any such delicacy), when she says to me, "Lee, you have to grow up and be a good looking man because you can't get any uglier than you are right now." This hits me hard and is the setting in of my inferiority complex that grows with each passing year.

The question of my veracity now arises. This is the first of the many times you will, with no doubt have questions about many of the episodes in my life. You will find it a little difficult to comprehend that, with all the childhood illnesses I have endured and overcome, that many of the

Irvin Boring

following events could have taken place. I want to stress the point that when I am sick, I am very, very sick and when I am between afflictions I am extremely healthy and strong, no matter how much my body is lacking flesh.

CHAPTER
5

CHILD HEROISM

Snow lies thick on the ground, and is even deeper in the forest where the trees prevent the penetration of the sun's rays. Rising temperatures and heavier than usual rain fall causes the snow to melt very fast, increasing the water flow in the stream where the boys of my neighborhood have our small swimming dam. This high, fast flowing water washes away the breast of the dam and erodes away the bank, rendering the location useless for rebuilding our dam.

We pick another spot upstream where it curves out from the foot of the hill enough to have a small level section of ground between it and the hill on the left side of the breast, when looking upstream. A large rock is located upstream from the breast right next to the right bank. When the breast is completed and the dam is filled with water this rock is completely submerged to where it is covered with about an inch and a half of water and the water is so murky the stone cannot be seen.

To the right of the dam and the submerged rock, the ground is level and has a tree growing about three feet from the water's edge. The first branch of this tree grows out horizontality from the trunk, parallel with the waters edge and is about four feet off the ground. I climb the tree and dive from this branch, propelling myself out enough to clear the unseen rock. In order to clear the rock I twist my body and hit the water sideways.

Johnny who is two years older than me says, "If you can do it I sure can."

I tell him, "Be sure you throw yourself out enough to clear the rock."

The rest of us are standing around our fire on the hill side of the dam, roasting our potatoes in the hot ashes, and watch as Johnny climbs out on the limb and makes his dive. All is well and good except for one thing; he makes his dive but instead of propelling himself out, he dives down at an angle with his arms spread out and extended over his head. His arms straddle each side of the rock and he hit's it dead center with the top of his head rendering him unconscious.

I run to the waters edge and dive, with enough momentum that my dive carries me to Johnny without having to swim. He is laying face down in the water and I pull him out onto the bank, lay him on his stomach, and see his scalp is split open right down the middle of the top of his head and someone exclaims, "Look, his brains are hanging out."

All the other kids are still standing around the fire so I call out, "Throw me a shirt." Someone grabs a white tee shirt, from a pile of cloth, runs across the breast and hands it to me. I am wrapping it around Johnny's head when he regains consciousness, but not his senses, and he jumps up and takes off running with the shirt hanging loose. It is a good thing he is one of the kids wearing cut off pants. He runs all the way to the area where he lives, but instead of going to his house, he goes to several of the neighbors, until one of them grabs hold of him and takes him home. Our potatoes never did get eaten.

Talking with Johnny later reveals he had not gone home in the first place because he feared another terrible beating from his father and the awful strict punishment from his mother. Fortunately his skull is not damaged and the greatest punishment he receives is the stitching of his scalp, with a needle and thread by his mother, without the use of a pain killer. Johnny goes around the neighborhood a long time with his head wrapped and the cut finally heals.

The hillside bank of Decker Avenue reservoir is very steep with a large tree growing about six feet up the bank from the waters edge. There is a heavy growth of wild grape vines hanging from its limbs so we cut a good heavy one and use it to swing out from the bank and drop or dive into the water from a height of about twenty feet, all the while on the lookout for the arrival of guards because swimming is prohibited.

Johnny swings out, drops into the water, goes under and surfaces swinging his arms, then goes under again. I am the youngest of the bunch and as they all stand around and watch, I dive in, swim out to the spot where Johnny went under, dive and am fortunate enough to grab him by his hair.

Pulling him to the surface, he gets a strangle hold around my neck, and I think I will drown before I break the hold and pull him to the bank by his hair. Others pull him from the water, lay him on his stomach with his head downhill on the steep bank and press on his back. Johnny has not gotten much water in his lungs so after spitting up a little it is not long before he is back to normal.

Johnny is a good swimmer so someone asks, "What happened?"

"I don't know. I just panicked."

Another voice tells him, "Go back in the water and swim."

"No, I'm afraid I'll drown," and he is reluctant to do so.

"We know you can do it so you're going back in the water," and we crowd around him forcing him down the bank, and into the water, where he takes a few practice strokes and he is right back at home in the water. I have saved Johnny's life for the second time.

Winter has just set in and experiencing a period of exceptionally good health I am into swimming at the Young Men's Christian Association, located in Johnstown, Pennsylvania two miles from my home. I don't know if swimming at the Y. M. C. A., then emerging into the freezing winter air and riding the trolley home has anything to do with it, but I develop a severe case of rheumatic fever. Our family doctor tells Mom and Dad, "My son has just joined me in my practice, so will it be alright if he treats Lee?" The doctor's son had the disease when he was a child, so in medical school he directed his studies to specialize in this illness and I am one of his first patients. He is a genius in my treatments, for after a couple of month in the hospital the large dark blue sores all over my body disappear. I lay in my hospital bed and listen as the doctor informs my parents, "Lee should take up a musical instrument because he will never be physically fit to lead a normal life. He must never exert or overheat himself."

Back at home I am once again faced with the task of learning to walk and I do all and everything I am not supposed to do to be a normal boy. It is miraculous how short of a period of time it takes until my body once again becomes strong, with lots of stamina, and I function normally.

CHAPTER
6

SWING SCYTHE

After repeating the eight grade due to my bout and hospitalization with the rheumatic fever it is summer school break in 1942, a little more than two month shy of my sixteenth birthday. With the miraculous recovery from my fever behind me, I stand about five feet nine and a half inches tall, weigh about one hundred and thirty pounds and I have so much energy that I have resumed my foraging of the forest for edible items. These excursions not only encompass the forest of Laurel Mountain above the cemetery, but is expanded a number of miles to the south.

Returning home from one of these sojourns into the woods, in mid afternoon I am following along the telephone line that runs between Johnstown, Pennsylvania and Pittsburgh, Pennsylvania. This right of way originates at the forest's edge, about a hundred yards up the hill in back of the one room, two class school house I attended for first and second grades. In my haste to get home I am running (as I usually do) when I encounter a crew of men, swinging scythes, just starting to clear the growth of grass, weeds and brush from the right-of-way.

Locating the foreman, I ask him to give me a job.

"How old are you?" He asks.

"I'm fifteen."

He stands there for a long time, (that to me seems like he is taking forever) scrutinizing me. A fifteen year old teenager, asking for a man's job. He asks me, "Have you ever swung a scythe?"

I tell him, "No, but I've seen it done on my uncles farm at haying time."

I guess I measure up because he says, "Aright, I'll give you a try, and he takes me to his company pickup truck and furnishes me with a scythe, a whetstone, and a pair of long handled twig cutters, telling me, "The job pays twenty three cents an hour. Don't let me down. Asking me my name, he write it down on a little pad and instructs me, "Go fill that gap over there on the right side of the line and pick up the routine." Placing the whetstone into my right pants pocket and placing one handle of the twig cutter under the back right hand side of my belt, and carrying the scythe I do as instructed and start swinging.

Dad's efforts at teaching me material things in life has paid off, because after a short observation of the men swinging and sharpening their scythes with the whetstone, I have no trouble picking up the procedure. There are small saplings sparsely growing in with the brush and grass so when the scythe blade strikes one of these saplings, it feels like my arms are being jerked right out of their shoulder sockets. If the sapling trunk is to large for the scythe to cut all the way through and the blade gets stuck. I jiggle it lose, remove the twig cuter from my belt, cut the sapling, and reinsert the cutter on my belt. As soon as I have taken the whetstone out of my pocket and have run it over the scythe blade to make sure it is nice and sharp, I resume my swing.

Getting home that evening I tell Mom the good news and she can not believe I have a job that pays more than my dad is earning working as a carpenter. In the following days, after swinging the scythe for eight hours, my arms are locked in the position of holding the scythe and will not straighten out, so I go home with my elbows locked in the position of holding the scythe. Mom applies cold wet towels around my elbows and wrists to get my arms to straighten out. Even though it is arm jarring and back breaking work, I stick it out and go to work every day.

My first pay check is for just a few hours and is right, but the check for my first full week of forty eight hours is not the same amount as the other workers. The foreman had told me the job paid twenty three cents an hour, so I go to the foreman in private and tell him, "You told me you would pay me twenty three cents an hour but this is not right, my check is for twelve dollars, ninety six cents more than the other men's pay checks." He informs me, "That's right; and be sure and keep this to yourself. The others are getting twenty three cents an hour, but you are outworking all the others, so I am paying you two cents an hour more." I have never earned any amount of money like this before and the foreman's words gives my ego a tremendous boost. As the days pass and the work become routine I have time to think.

One summer I earned a few dollars picking strawberries on the strawberry farm in Westmont for which I received two cents a quart. Another summer I worked as a farm hand on a farm up on Laurel Mountain for fifty cents a week, plus my lunch. One week the woman I worked for gives me a fifty cent bonus for the week because I am such a good worker, and the next week it is a different story. It is during the dog days of summer, and with the bright, blistering sun beating down on me and the stifling hot air I am breathing as I hoe and pull weeds from the garden rows, I guess I have taken too many water breaks, for the farming woman informs me, "You are no longer needed because you are just a lazy no good kid." This news devastates both me and Mom, but I guess the lady was right in her reasoning, for it is just a short period of time until I am hospitalized with one of my illnesses. I had probably been getting weaker and weaker without realizing it.

Blackberries and blueberries that I picked up on Laurel Mountain, I sold door to door in Morrellville for ten cents a quart. I also made a little money by growing leaf lettuce and green onions in a plot in a neighbor's garden, then each bunch I sold brought in ten cents.

I did anything to make a little money. I picked through the trash in the dump up on Mountain Road, saving any metal, paper, and glass I found. Separating the glass by color I broke it up and put it into any containers I could find and hauled it all home in my little wagon. Every so often a junkman came by with his horse and wagon and bought these items from me for a few cents. This venture came to an abrupt end when our next-door neighbor came and told Dad, "I have been getting things from the dump for a long time and I consider that by Lee picking through the dump for things is stealing from me." Without a word of arguing with the man Dad tells me, *"Take all the stuff you gathered from the dump to the man's yard and don't go picking through the dump again."* This devastates me but without question I do whatever Dad tells me and I do so with a broken heart

Mom arouses me around three thirty each morning and I walk to Morrellville, where the Johnstown tribune has bundles of newspapers waiting for me in front of the Realto Movie Theater. After taking time to roll the papers, I place them in two newspaper carrier bags, sling the bag straps over my head, leaving a bag hanging on each side of my body, then I make the rounds of my newspaper route that encompasses about a three mile circle.

Answering the knock on our kitchen door on the afternoon of December 7,1941, I find the newspaper distributor standing there. We do not have a telephone so he has come to my home to have me go into Morrellville and sell a late, special edition of the paper, with large headlines, *"JAPS BOMB PEARL HARBOR."* At this time, we are experiencing a severe snow storm with snowflakes about the size of a nickel, so I dress as warm as I can and he drops me, and my papers off, on the main street, Fairfield Avenue. I travel up one street and down another, yelling at the top of my voice, *"Extra, extra read all about it, Japs bomb Pearl Harbor."* The residents who hear my call, come flocking out of their houses and buy the newspaper. To compensate me for selling these papers I had been given ten extra newspapers to sell and keep the money. Well, let me tell you, I sold out in a very short time. I have made fifty cents for about two hours work.

War is raging in Europe and the United State is very much involved, so every man eighteen years of age and older has to register for the draft. The Draft Board figures working out in the forest is a good place for draft dodgers to hide so they send a team to the sight where my crew is clearing the right-of-way in hopes of catching one. Work is disrupted and the scythe swingers are lined up and each man has to show his draft registration papers. The foreman is very unhappy at this work stoppage, but there is nothing he can do.

I have not gotten in line and I am standing off to the side, and when the last man is checked the official calls out, "What's the matter with you fella, why didn't you get in line? Come over here," Standing in front of the two officials, I am told to produce my draft card. I tell them, "I don't know what you are talking about."

Hearing these words, the faces of both officials light up, knowing their trip to the right-of-way has paid off. They know they have a catch. One of them makes the remark, "Boy, we have a live one here. We finally caught a draft dodger," and asks me, "Just what is your standing with the draft board?" When I tell them I have not registered for anything they demand to see some identification, which of course I do not have to produce.

One of them finally asks, "How old are you."

I reply, "Fifteen:"

They look at me dumb founded and one of them remarks, "You have got to be lying. Come with us."

They take me to my home and Mom vouches for my age.

One of the officials remarks to Mom, "We are amazed your son is doing such a manly work at his age."

I am returned back to the work site where the foreman is so glad to get me back that he lets slip to the draft board team, "I'm glad you brought him back because he is such a good worker I pay him two cents an hour more than the others." If he thought his day was bad, because of the work delay, he probably hoped he was dead for uttering these words.

Hearing this remark, the entire crew of grown men, are so angry at finding out a kid is being paid more than they are, that they all quit on the spot.

One man asks me, "If I can make a deal with the foreman to pay us ten dollars for each section we clear will you work with me on a fifty-fifty split?" I know he is a good hard worker so I promptly reply, "Yes I will."

The Foreman agrees to his proposal so the next morning we continue to clear. We clear two sections a day, with a section extending from one pole to the next, resulting in each of us earning ten dollars a day. This is an enormous amount of money for any working man, and here I am just a kid making all this money. We do this until just before the end of my summer break, but, alas all good things must end. Our clearing just two sections a day is an effort in futility, and is not making a dent in the right of way. The phone company hires crop dusters to fly over the right of way and spray the foliage with an orange colored defoliant that kills everything that grows, so our services are no longer needed.

CHAPTER
7

DROP OUT

I am afraid I have not been completely truthful with you, for earlier I stated, "I can overcome any and all diversities." The year I enter the ninth grade, I am several years behind my peers due to missing a couple of school years because of all my illnesses. I am still a dunce and the state of my mind is such that, the one affliction I have not overcome is my inferiority complex that is at its apex. It has grown to the point I cannot face a group of people.

When choosing my ninth grade classes I am told that public speaking is a mandatory class. Forget it. When I get up in front of the class my body literally foams with perspiration from the fear of people looking at me and this is more than I can bear. After several attempts at getting up in front of the class to speak, I find my body is all wet with perspiration and I stumble through a couple of words and I have to give it up. Three weeks after my sixteenth birthday I drop out of school.

Thank God I have sense enough to sign up for trade school through the National Youth Association, "N. Y.

A." In trade school I am in my element and find my niche during welding training, because in a solitary booth with my welding helmet down I have no one but myself to contend with, so I feel I am sitting in paradise. I believe it is at this stage of my life that a transformation starts to occur and I see that where most of the other welding trainees struggle, I excel. I start building up my self esteem.

Representatives from Baldwin Locomotive Works, in Eddystone, Pennsylvania, come to Westmont where the welding school is located to administer welding tests to the students who have completed the twelve week course. I am six weeks into the course and progressing so well, the instructor talks them into letting me take the test.

Six of us out of the thirty five students perform with enough satisfaction to be hired for a job that requires leaving home and moving two hundred and fifty miles to Chester, Pennsylvania, to work in the Baldwin Locomotive Works Defense Plant, located in Eddystone, Pennsylvania.

The six of us make the move, and after a few weeks we all come down with severe cases of homesickness so the other five all quit and return home. My willpower permits me to overcome the homesickness, so at just a few months past my sixteenth birthday I am living alone in a hotel room on the second floor of the Chelsea Hotel, on Second Street, in Chester, Pennsylvania. Being so young I am a novelty for the patrons of the lounge and they all treat me like a son.

In the factory I again excel, for when my fellow workers as a group are to be chastised for sloppy work, the foreman comes to me and says, "Lee, I have no complaint about the quality of your work. I can't show favoritism, so you have to attend the briefing with everyone else, though it is not meant for you." I am the youngest individual working in the plant, earning a man's wages. I am exceeding the performance of all the others and I am accepted as a man. This kicks my ego up another another notch and my inferiority complex starts receding.

The plant built and modifies the armies Sherman tanks and one of my jobs is electric welding additional armor plating, one and a half inch thick, onto crucial points of the tanks where occupants are most vunerable. All the welds are x-rayed and not one of mine is ever found defective. Retain this point of welding on tanks because it comes up later.

I have so much time on my hands, that the days seem to never end so I go to the Young Men's Christian Association building just down the street from the Chelsea hotel where I have my room and inquire of the manager, "May I use your gym and swimming pool?"

He informs me, "Not very many peoples use them, and you have to use the buddy system."

"I have no buddies and I will be coming in at odd hours."

"Gee, I don't know if I can let you in alone? I might get in deep trouble, so show me if you can handle yourself okay."

After demonstrating to him that I am part fish in the pool and that I am very agile in the gym he gives me my own personal key with the instructions, "If there is no one using the facilities when you leave, be sure to turn out the lights and lock the gym door."

I do not encounter another living soul in the pool so I swim continuously lap after lap. The basketball court has a circular running track built high up around the walls, with sloping corners so I can keep up my speed as I run for hours.

There are three heavy ropes hanging from the ceiling with knots tied in them every foot. They are out of the basketball court boundaries and I grab hold of the ropes, stick my feet straight out and ascend and descend them time after time.

There is no diving board in the pool so I utilize the gym's horse vault spring board to practice my diving summersaults. I improve my skill to where I can land, both feet and head first, by tumbling on the floor matt as I land. Because of the broad field of exercising my body develops into what you call raw bone muscles; they do not bulge.

I eat all my meals in a diner and I order complete meals from the menu. When I am finished eating there are items of food I do not like left on my plate. A motherly waitress asks, "Why did you leave these peas and carrots on your plate?"

I tell her, "I do not like peas and carrots."

She informs me, "Why pay for something you are not going to eat? Never order a full meal if there is an item on it you do not intend to eat, always ask for a substitute item or order individual items." From then on I heed her advice and never leave any uneaten food on my plate.

The Navy is taking young men at the age of seventeen so I go to the recruiting office to enlist. Telling the recruiter,

"I want to join the Navy." The first thing he does is tell me, "Okay." He hands me a 3x5 card and tells me, "Look through that doorway, cover your right eye with the card and read the fourth line of the eye chart on the far wall."

I get a sinking feeling in the pit of my stomach because my left eye is my weak eye and I know I am doomed before I start, but I do as the recruiter instructs me.

"I cannot read it," I say.

"Read the third line."

"I cannot read it."

"Read the second line."

"I cannot see it."

"Read the big, E."

Straining my eye I tell him, "It is just a blur and I cannot make it out."

He tells me, "Thank you. We cannot use you. Goodbye and good luck." This is as close as I get to being a sailor.

CHAPTER
8

BACK HOME TO JOHNSTOWN

Walking into the office of Baldwins, five weeks shy of my eighteenth birthday, I inform the office manager, "I will be quitting my job in thirty days." I am informed, "You can't quit your job because of the Wartime Man Power Act." The manager expounds on this by telling me, "This Act states, (not a direct quote), If one quits a critical job he will not be permitted to take another job for a period of six month. One other thing; we have been getting you deferred every six months. If you stay with us you will never have to enter the service. If you quit you will be drafted immediately." The last part of the managers statement gives me a feeling of elation, for it would fulfill my dream of being in the service, and I say, "That cannot be, because I am not of draft age." A week before my eighteenth birthday I follow through with my notice and return to my parent's home in Johnstown, Pennsylvania.

Instead of just laying around waiting for a job to materialize, I spend my time by helping Dad do his small carpentry jobs. On my eighteenth birthday, June 30, 1944, I make a trip to the Selective Service Office and register for the draft. Wanting to be in the service so badly, I put it into writing that I do not want to be classified, but instead I want to be inducted and sent right through.

As soon as I finish registering, I proceed directly to the Bethlehem Steel Corporation, Employment Office, to apply for a job as a welder. Sitting at a table and filling out the job application form I remind myself, "Do not let it slip that you worked at Baldwin's." Scanning my application the clerk breaks out in laughter and announces to all her coworkers, "Everybody come and look at this." All assemble at the counter and my application is passed around. Seeing it is my eighteenth birthday and applying for a job as a journeyman welder gives them all a good laugh.

When the application form makes it's rounds of the office and is returned to the clerk processing it, she says to me, "There is no way anyone can be a full fledged welder at such a young age, it takes years to become a first class welder." Persisting with my claim, that I am a journeyman welder the clerk asks, "Just who do you think you are, coming in here and making such an outlandish claim? Are you for real? We have an excellent three year apprenticeship program that you can apply for."

With me still persisting and not backing down, she finely decides to humor me and asks, "Do you have any relatives working for the Company?"

I tell her, "My father, Joseph Boring works in the Railroad Car Shop."

She phones the plant and instructs me, "Have a seat until your dad can be put on the phone."

After about a half hour the clerk summons me and tells me, "Wait while I consult with my supervisor." When the clerk returns and I am again at the counter she informs me, "It has been arranged, that if you can pass the welding certification test and the physical, we will waver the apprenticeship and the age rule and hire you."

The company officials involved are so impressed with me, they furnish a company limousine, and transport me the two miles, to where the test is administered. Passing it with such ease, I think, "This must be some kind of a joke." I am taken back to the employment office where the company physician performs a brief physical. Having fulfilled the two specified requirements, I am hired on the spot, so you see, my persistence does pay off. I really should have informed the clerk about my deal with the draft board, but hadn't.

With the instructions from the clerk; "At 6 o'clock tomorrow morning report to the office of the Railroad Car Shop in Franklin, where you took the welding test and be sure to have your welding equipment with you." I go home and start my wait to hear from the draft board. When Dad comes home from work I ask him, "What did you tell the clerk?"

"The foreman didn't like me going off the production line to talk on the phone but I told the woman, "If he says he is a first class welder, believe him.""

The next morning at seven o'clock I start my new welding job and compared to earning $10.50 for an eight hour shift welding tanks in the defense plant, the first day welding railroad cars, I earn a lucrative wage of $18.

ξ TRAINING FOR WAR ₹

CHAPTER
9

ADJUSTING TO ARMY LIFE

My wait to hear from the draft board lasts four weeks, when I receive notification by mail to report to the Induction Center in Pittsburgh, Pennsylvania, on August 5, 1944, to take my induction physical. The envelope I receive also contains a round trip train ticket, so with envelope in hand, I make the trip with great apprehensions for I had failed the navy physical so miserably.

It seems I have weathered the storm in my struggle to survive health wise, for it has been four years since I have suffered any illnesses. My biggest worry is, "Will I pass the eye test?" My right eye is 20/15 and my left eye is just under the legally blind status so I do a little cheating; I give close attention to the line of the chart, the men ahead of me in line are asked to read. Memorizing these lines of letters on the eye chart with my right eye I am able to respond with the correct letters when asked to read the chart with my left eye.

Being handed my physical papers upon completion of the physical, I see that I stand five feet, ten inches tall and I weigh one hundred and forty pounds. Passing the physical gives me a feeling of great joy; I believe this day is the happiest day of my life because I have become a man, equal to every one else. The reason I feel so elated is the fact that, suffering so many illnesses as a youngster, I did not believe I would ever physically qualify to enter the military.

With the physical behind me I move on to the row of tables, manned by recruiters representing the different branches of the military to be interviewed as to which branch of the service I prefer. The table I sit down at is manned by a marine recruiter, who sounds so sincere in trying to persuade, (he practically begs,) me to sign up with the marines. When he finally convinces me, and I agree to be a marine, he picks up a huge stamp and slams it down on my papers. When he hands the paper to me, there it is in black and white, "United States Army."

Departing the induction center, I am in possession of orders and a one way train ticket in hand to report to Cumberland Gap Army Base, in Maryland on 9 August 1945, for processing. Being employed for less than five weeks, I notify Bethlehem Steel that I have been inducted into the army. They wish me good luck and assure me my job with them will be available when I return from the service.

Aside from the hustle bustle wait, hustle bustle wait while processing at Cumberland Gap, I learn a valuable lesson about the Army. I notice a loose screw on one of the brackets that holds the window screen. I happen to have a screw driver in my possession so I get it out and commence to tighten the screw. A civilian gentleman with a tool belt around his waist happens to come by at this time. Seeing what I am doing he approaches me and informs me in no uncertain terms, "What the hell are you doing, trying to knock me out of a job? Don't let me catch you doing anything like this again." Lesson learned; no matter how minute, in the army, never do anything unless you are told or ordered to do it.

Another notable day of my life is 12 August, 1944, when I and thousands of others, from all walks of life, converge at Camp Blanding, Florida, to begin army basic training. Upon arrival we are assigned to companies, platoons etc., and then barracks. Of all the recruits who make up my training company, I am the youngest at just five weeks into my eighteenth year.

At this point in my narrations I find it very difficult to keep things in any chronological order and still give you, the reader, a true understanding of the character of this young recruit. After a few days of settling in, as with all gatherings of people, groups of friends are established. Despite my being the youngest individual of my training company, (most likely in all of the camp), I am accepted in all the groups. One of the things that make me acceptable to all these people is that they consider me very congenial, a characteristic trait in me that is so bizarre that it must be clarified.

As you recall, just two years prior to this, I had to drop out of school due to my severe inferiority complex.

In this two year period I have developed both mentally and physically, beyond my wildest dreams.

A young man from Brooklyn has much more street smarts than any of the rest of us, and he could be very popular, except for the fact that his attitude is all wrong. Every decision he makes is strictly for his own benefit, with no regard as to how it affects the rest of us. Everyone admires the way he weasels out of distasteful duties that the rest of us are ordered to perform. He knows just when to have stomach cramps, a sever headache, or some kind of virus that gets him excused from unpopular details. He has a multitude of admirers but is lacking respect from any one of his fellow trainees, any of the cadre, non commissioned officers, as well as any of the training officers.

It takes only a few days for the homesickness to hit just about everyone in our training company but me, so when most of the others get to the point of crying I am there to give counsel and ease their state of mind. Remember, two years earlier just after leaving home, "*I had the fortitude to overcome the terrible feeling of homesickness.*"

As with all recruits, I make my share of goofs, and break the rules along with everyone else. The next day, standing at attention before the company commander, each criminal in turn is asked, "What is your excuse for your actions?" When the others attempt to justify their goofs by making excuses for their mistakes, I tell the person judging us, "Yes Sir, I goofed, and I am afraid the others were depending on me, and I have let them down. I influenced the others so I will take the responsibility for our errors," (another of my characteristics).

An example of this is; in the evenings as we sit in the company day room writing letters home, in our exuberance we sometimes lose track of time causing us to linger over our writings until it is past the time of, "bed check." The next day when we are standing before the company commander, and it is my turn to be dealt with he asks me, "What is your excuse?" I respond, "Sir, I have no excuse, and I am afraid the others were depending on me to keep track of the time and get them to bed before lights out. I take the responsibility for all of us missing bed check so I will take the punishment for us all." The captain stares at me as if he can not believe he is hearing right and exclaims, "It doesn't work that way, every one is responsible for his own actions, so each must be punished." I am given double the punishment the others receive but gain the respect of all, including the captain.

One evening, not many days into basic training, as we sit in the post exchange drinking our 3.2 beer, a fellow trainee says to me, "You are the first really true person any of us have ever met. When you laugh your whole face lights up making the happiness contagious, and when you speak it seems to be with complete honesty."

The dairies up grade their delivery wagons to trucks, and I get a job on one of them as a delivery boy, working before going to school. I am not too bright so one morning when I run a bottle of milk to a house, the lady stops me, hands me a nickel and tells me, "Give this to the milkman to pay up my bill." Like the dummy I am, I put it in my pocket and keep it. When the milkman attempts to collect this nickel from the lady she tells him, "I gave the nickel to your delivery boy," and I deny it, so he fires me. This is a wake up call for me and from then on I make every effort to be completely honest.

I buy five quarts of engine oil at an automotive parts store, and when I get home and look at the sales slip I see I have been charged for only four. Returning to the store with the sales slip I explain to the clerk, "I bought five quarts of oil but you only charged me for four." When the other quart is paid for, the clerk remarks, "This has never happened to me before, I have never heard of such honesty."

The barracks have a one tier, single shelf with a cloth rod mounted under it for everyone's use, extending along the walls of the barracks just under the oblong windows located all around the top of the walls. Because of the hanging cloth, the metal framed cots around the outer perimeter of the floor are single, with folding metal frames and are placed with one side of each cot next to the wall. The center of the floor accommodates two rows of double deck beds with their head and foot facing lengthwise of the one large room of the barracks. I am fortunate enough to have my single deck cot just inside the door along the wall with the head frame next to the door and when I have the opportunity, I lay relaxed, with my booted feet sticking through the folding metal foot frame.

I am laying so, when a buddy enters through the door, says, "Get up!" and playfully lifts up on the head frame of my cot causing the foot frame to fold on my shins. I do some yelping for a while because his reaction is to drop the cot, which only causes it to fold more, and there I am helpless until he finally picks the head of the cot all the way up to vertical and releases the pressure on my shins enough for me to step out from between the frame. Attempting to relieve the pain by rubbing the sore spots reveals a large indent in each of my shin bones.

Short sheeting someone's bed is more work and effort than you may think anyone would do for a laugh. For those of you who are not familiar with this prank, it is accomplished by striping off the blanket and the top sheet of a bed. Once you have removed the blanket and top sheet a great length of the removed sheet is tucked under the mattress at the head, then the sheet is doubled back about mid way of the bed. The blanket is put back on and finally the sheet is folded over the edge of the blanket to make it look normal.

When the master of the bed slips under the sheet and blanket expecting to stretch out and relax, his feet are brought up short and it is a terrible feeling, until it sinks in, "You have been short sheeted." You might be short sheeted, because you are a pain to others, or just the opposite, you are a nice guy. The pain ones, can not take this lightly and raise all kinds of hell when it happened to them, so they are repeat recipients and every one but them gets a good laugh.

When the good guys get the treatment he just exclaims, "Well god damn!" and everyone including him laughs. Since he did not get irritated there is no sense in repeating. The one and only time it happens to me, I just peel back the edge of the sheet and slip under the blanket with no fuss.

I will not bore you with all the rhetoric of the food served in the army, but I will say this, "I never met a meal I did not like." The most famous of army food, "chow," in army talk is creamed beef on toast, better known as S. O. S. I claim to have never had my stomach full up to this point in my life so, with my ravenous appetite, at meal times I am always close to the head of the chow line waiting for the mess hall door to be opened.

Going through the serving line, the food is portioned out moderately so everyone will be fed. With my tray loaded with all the food the servers pile on it I move to a table and consume the food. When everything has vanished from my tray I sit and wait for the call of "seconds" to be announced, and then I go back through the line and am served again. Once more I wait and if there is any food left the call for thirds goes out and I am right there. I am in hog's heaven and figure where else in the world can you consume all the food you can hold and all for free? I am so active that I still do not put on any weight.

A group of us are sitting in the post exchange one evening, unwinding after a hard day of training; that is everyone is unwinding but me, for I have yet to get up tight about any aspects of our training. As we are drinking good cold 3.2 beer, one buddy says, "Lee, you seem to have a lot of street smarts and we all look up to you and we sort of follow your lead. You handle everything much better than the rest of us, keep us going and raise our spirits. How can you take all this harassment and rigor in stride with such ease, when it is pure torture for the rest of us? Because we all look up to you for guidance, we have talked it over and decided, if you don't mind we want to call you, "Mister Lee. Is that all right with you?" From then on I am, "Mister Lee."

The cadre hears me being addressed as "Mister Lee" by my buddies, and my actions so far has gained their respect so they pick up on it and finally the officers follow suit. You think, "This sounds very unorthodox." I believe at this point in the army I lose my identity when they dub me, because from then on private Boring is only heard at roll calls and musters. I do not realize it at the time but accepting this misnomer burdens me with great responsibilities.

This episode is so unbelievable, I do not think any military man who has experienced basic training, will accept it as the truth. When there is a decision to be made that will affect the whole company Mister Lee is summoned and asked his opinion as to what action I think should be taken. Here is an example. Our activities are about to be concluded for the day and we are a great distance from the barracks. One of the cadres non commissioned officers orders me, "Report to the company commander:" I think, "Oh Lord, now what have I done?"

Standing before him, the captain gives me this speech, "Mister Lee, the men have one of two choices they can make. One, they can march back to the barracks, get in late, have a late supper, get up extra early in the morning and march back out here. Or two; they can stay here, and I will have the kitchen mess truck bring supper out, they can sleep here in the field and have breakfast brought out. Poll them and see which they prefer?" I reply, "Sir, it needs no polling, I feel I can speak for them all, we will stay here," and that's the action that is taken.

I am sitting on the kitchen table, watching mom mixing bread dough. For some inadvertent reason I scoot off the table, unfortunately landing on our beautiful pet kitten's head, causing both of its eyes to pop out and hang down its face. When I see what has happened I am nauseated at the sight, but taking quick action I swoop the poor thing up and run outside to the yard, lay it on a 2x4, and hit it a deadly blow with another 2x4.

I feel terrible but it is something that had to be done, and I have done it. I get a shovel, carry the kitten's body and the shovel away from the house, dig a small hole and give it a proper funeral, all the while having tears run down my cheeks. This incident is the first one in my life where if I encounter a crisis, I can make a decision, take charge of myself and get the task done.

CHAPTER
10

PHYSICAL TRAINING

The muscles in my body are in such excellent condition that I am bored with all aspects of the training, consisting of anything physical, so it is a cake walk for me.

A family living one block down, the steep assent, and on the other side of Ash Road from my home, have a two car garage and a model T Ford. The car is never kept in the garage so the boys of the family who are all young men utilize it as a boxing arena. The brothers have several pairs of large boxing gloves on hand, and any boy who is unlucky enough to pass the garage at the wrong time is caught, dragged into the garage and adorned with a pair of these gloves. He is then forced to defend himself as he is given boxing lessons, like it or not. I dread passing by this hellish garage, for when two boys are caught, they are both fitted with a pair of these gloves, and if they are reluctant to fight, the brothers grab each boy by the arms, and hit the other boy until he gets his dander up. When the boy being hit is tired of all these blows his anger takes over and he returns the blows on his own.

Since I am the youngest and smallest boy in the neighborhood I am chopped liver for the bigger ones. I am much shorter and skinnier than the others boys so I take some terrible beatings, but I am so agile, with each event I become more combatant and aggressive until I soon am able to hold my own. Eventually I start outlasting some of the bigger boys.

I am twelve years old and walking home on the sidewalk of Fairfield Avenue, passing through Morrellville when I encounter a girl on the sidewalk in tears. There is a boy about two years older and quite a bit heavier than me standing in front of her. Betty is in tears so I ask her, "Why are you crying, Betty?"

She tells me "He is picking on me and he won't stop."

"Why don't you just go in the house?"

"I don't want to go in,"

I say to the boy, "Stop teasing her."

"You little punk. Who do you think is going to make me?"

"I am!" and I tear into him.

I believe he is so surprised that such a small kid would take him on that I am getting the better of him and after a while he gasps, "Stop!"

I tell him, "From now on you have a little more respect for the girls."

Betty says, "Thank you Pee Wee," and I continue home.

The next day, being a Sunday, Dad is home and in the yard sharpening a hand saw. I am watching him when the boy and his father come into the yard. The man says, "Joe, my boy tells me your boy, Pee Wee, beat him up yesterday for no reason and I don't believe him, because Pee Wee is so small. Do you agree with me that we have to make men of our boys so they don't grow up to be wimps? I want to teach my boy to never back down from anyone, so I want him and Pee Wee to have it out again."

"Of course. I teach my boys the same," Dad answers. "Lee, did you fight him and tell me why?"

"He was picking on Betty, "B", and dared me to stop him."

"You shouldn't have interfered because it was none of your business. Do you think you can whip him again?"

"I don't want to fight him."

"That's not what I asked you. Do you think you can whip him?"

"Yes," I answer.

"Then do it," Dad tells me.

I tear into the boy and am getting the better of him when his dad says, "That's enough. I just wanted to make sure my boy would put up a fight. Pee Wee, you sure surprise me. Joe, I hope there is no hard feeling over this. Now let's all shake hands and put this behind us." The boy is reluctant but comes around and we all shake. Dad and the man get together and talk just like the friends they are. My punishment for fighting in the first place is to fight again.

I hear so much, "Hut, two, three four, hut, two, three four, etc.," that it seems like we are drilling or participating in a forced march every few days.

During the times I am afflicted with one of my sicknesses, I am either in the hospital or I am too weak to do anything. In between ailments I am extremely healthy and strong so I am permitted to do things with the older boys.

We go over the ridge of Laurel Mountain, veer left, travel quite a ways then cross back over the ridge and make our way to a cabin called, "Salt Block." We have one huge nap sack between us and take turns carrying it. When we make this trek in knee deep snow I have to prove to myself I have the grit to participate, so I break trail most of the way. By the time we arrive at the cabin I can hardly walk because of the soreness in my groin, but I will never admit it is too much for me.

During the summer we load the napsack with food and take turns carrying it as we trek up the Mountain Road, cross the ridge of Laurel Mountain and descend the other slope until we come to the Haws Pike. Here we make a right and follow the pike along the Conemaugh River. We pass through the small community of New Florence and walk by Seward, then around the base of Laurel Mountain. About mid way of the seven mile trek to Oakhurst, we stop and freshen up. We do this by drinking good cold water from an old rusted tin cup that is ever present hanging from a spike driven into the cement around the pipe sticking out of the uphill bank of the Pike.

Now we cross the pike, and descend the bank to a dam that has its breast about fifteen feet from the cement arch over the water that extends back under the highway. There is no outlet at the back of the dam and the sun never hits this area, so the water is so icy cold, when we jump in we have to get out fast.

Some of us continue down the bank to the round wooden tank atop of about twenty foot timbers. This tank is filled with water by gravity from the dam and is used to fill the water compartments of the railroad locomotive tenders.

Climbing the ladder we look over the edge and if the tank is full we slip over the edge and swim. We are swimming in about thirty feet of water that is not as cold as the water in the dam and if anyone hears a train we scramble from the tank and make tracks back up to the water pipe. We are just kids, but we understand the peril we would be in if we are caught in the tank and the water level dropped as the tender of the locomotive is filled.

We eat, we drink some more water, then we resume our trek until we come to the city limits of Oakhurst, where we make a right and travel around the side of the mountain to home. The distance from New Florence to Oakhurst is a little over ten miles, so I figure we travel well over thirty mile in all.

There are several events that took place in my youth that attributes to my being able to excel in all aspects of the water exercises I encounter in our training. *It is a nice warm summer day right after my second birthday when dad says, "Come on, Lee, it's time you learned to swim, "and the two of us walk to the Chandler Avenue Reservoir. Standing on the dam side of the cement spillway, Dad picks me up, says, "Swim out by dog paddling" and then he throws me out over the water as far as he can. Hitting the water I sink to the bottom, come to rest on the sloping cement of the spillway and am able to hold my breath long enough to crawl up the slope and out at Dad's feet. He picks me up again and repeats, "You don't crawl out, you swim out," and he throws me in again. This time as soon as I hit the water I am able to dog paddle back to Dad, and the process is repeated. Later I wonder; "was dad really trying to teach me to swim?"*

My search for food takes me farther and farther into the forest. I run and I run; so this morning after crossing the summit of Laurel Mountain, I am descending the slope on the other side when I come across a small stream that is not more than a foot across and two inches deep. Because the slope is quit steep, the water flow is very fast and as I follow along it down stream, I come to a flat area of ground about eight feet long. I see this flat spot contains a hole in the stream that is about three feet wide and perhaps six feet long and I can see the walls of the hole are vertical but I can not make out its depth.

Shedding my clothes and entering the water I find it is very cold, is chest deep and the current is too swift for me to swim because my feet stay against the outlet wall. With my feet pushed against the ground at the outlet, I try swimming using the free style, but I can not swim fast enough to pull my feet away from the stream outlet wall to kick. I push off with my legs and kick my feet and swim with all my might but I keep drifting back.

Each time I return to my swimming hole and get into the water I keep up my attempts to kick, eventually building up my arm muscles to the point that my feet pull away from the outlet, and I lay there swimming with all my might, with my arm stroke and my feet kicking. I now am able to maintain my position in the middle of the pool. This is strenuous on me but I get stronger and stronger with each session.

Although my body is just skin and bones, I am all energy and after running the several miles to the hole I swim, then I leisurely make my way back through the forest eating as many of the fore mentioned wild edibles I come across. By the time I get home I am ravished and eat a large meal.

I am two months past my sixteenth birthday and the weather is so hot and muggy it is hard to breathe, so several of us teenagers go to the community swimming pool to cool off. Arriving at the pool we find a sign hanging at the gate opening displaying the words, "Closed for the swimming meet." The attendant sitting at a table tells us, "This swim meet is for adults and the only way to get in is to enter a swimming race." I say to my friends, "I'm hot and want to get in the water so I am going to sign up." I am the only one in the bunch to sign up for the free style race and I am admitted.

The pool is circular, two hundred feet in diameter, has a square platform in the middle supporting two, one meter diving boards and has a high diving tower sticking up in its middle. All the participants line up around the cement edge of the pool, and as the only youngster in the lineup I get a lot of banter from the grownups for thinking I can compete with them.

Instructions are given; "Dive in at the sound of the starting pistol and the first one to touch the pier wins." It just happens that I am the first one to touch the edge of the platform so I am proclaimed the winner. At the table on the way out I am presented with a blue ribbon that states, "Fichtner POOL, SWIMMING CARNIVAL, August 31, 1942, Senior Free Style (100Ft.) 1ˢᵗ place, LEE BORING."

The last but not least of the events is my swimming sessions at the Y. M. C. A.'s swimming pool.

While so many of the recruits struggle to get through all the different aspects of the obstacles course, it is routine for me because I have encountered and experienced, (to a certain degree) each and every one of the obstacles and hazards. I list just a few of these that deserve honorable mention. Many trainees lose their grip on the rope when swinging across water hazards but I have no problems because: *Two or three children, (myself included,) go into the forest above the cemetery where the trees have an extremely heavy amount of wild grapevines that have grown up into the tree branches. Locating trees that are on a steep slope we cut the vine up from the ground as far as we can reach, then pull the hanging vine uphill, get a good tight grip on the vine and swing out to great heights above the slope of the ground. If we are above a nice tree, we sometimes release our grip on the vine and drop down into the tree top.*

Swinging out on a freshly cut vine, I have just attained the peak of my swing, when the wet sap of the vine causes me to lose my grip and I fall. I do not know how many feet I drop but I come to a stop on the ground on my left side against the base of a tree trunk. Luckily for me I hit the tree with my stomach and my body sort of wraps around the trunk. The wind is knocked out of me so I lay there for a while gasping for breath. The Lord is looking out for a poor ignorant child, for had I hit the tree trunk with my back it would surely have snapped my spine.

The woods above the cemetery has a good saturation of trees, so us boys see who can travel the furthest distance without touching the ground. We do this by climbing a tree, work our way out on a limb as far as we can go, then jump to a branch of an adjoining tree. Working our way to the tree's trunk, we go through the routine all over again. One time I make my jump, and failing to firmly grab the tree limb, I fall, I don't know how many feet to the ground, landing flat on my back. I do not get knocked out but a thousand bright stars keep flashing in my head.

It is an unspoken creed among our tough bunch of rural neighborhood boys, that if you have a mishap, you do not just give up, you go right back and try again. As soon as I recover from my fall, I climb the tree from which I fallen and make another jump. This time if I execute my jump and fall, I will be prepared to tumble as I hit the ground. Making my jump I have no problem grabbing hold of the targeted branch.

This one vine we have cut is hanging from a huge tree that sits about fifteen feet up the steep bank on the uphill side of Mountain Road. The earth has been dug away for the road so the bank is too steep to climb. As we swing out across the road it is breath taking, for we are now about sixty or more feet above the sharp dropping down hill side of the road. We are all naive enough to think that if we lose our grip and fall, we will land in the top of the crab apple trees growing on the down hill slope. We can thank the lord for not making any one of us experience this fall.

I am in constant trouble with my parents, who repeatedly scold me for climbing up the rain spout on the corner of our house, getting onto the roof, then jumping off, tumbling as I make contact with the ground. They are so afraid that on one of these stunts, I will injure myself.

When we managed to get any time off from our training all the other trainees lay around the barracks, doctoring the enormous blisters on their feet and resting their sore muscles. I, on the other hand, have no blisters or muscle pain and need exercise. Therefore I run on the street of our billeting area out onto the paved highway, where I

run for about five miles, then I run back to the barracks.
I figure I have run approximately ten miles.

*I form a sort of cradle on one end of a stiff length of
straight wire, that I use to propel a large wire ring. It is great
fun for me to chase this ring all around the neighborhood; I
must run five miles a day and never get tired. With all this
running one would think I would develop blisters from my
shoes rubbing my feet, but not to worry because I wear no
shoes. All the boys in my neighborhood go shoeless and we
develope thick tough soles of our feet and heels.*

*Our gang of boys play this stupid idiotic game of
"Chicken," consisting of a thick spreading of broken up Coke
bottles and glass bottles we have found. When all this glass is
piled thick, each boy in the group is dared to walk across this
broken glass with all the jagged edges. If he refuses to walk he
is called Chicken. If he makes the walk and draws blood, he
is taunted with the words, "Sissy Pants." This is a cruel game
but none of the walkers obtains serious cuts because we are
one tough bunch.*

Crawling under barbed wire, strung across a field is quite
a task for most trainees, and the sounds made by the
machine guns firing live ammunitions over our heads
puts fear in my fellow trainee's hearts. I have no problems
with this because, as a child I had been exposed to live
ammunition being fired at me.

*Johnny J., who lives one block up the hill from me and
does not fit in with the other kids, is a loner and carries a
22 pistol. At the lower end of the sloping field area of the
cemetery not yet being used there is a wagon lane separating
the field from people's yards. Some of these yards have solid
wooden fences and as I walk or run by these fences, Johnny*

sits at the upper end of the field and shoots as close to me as he can without hitting me. The 22 slugs hit the fence just as in the background in a shooting gallery. I am sure he does the same with other kids and it is amazing no one ever gets hit.

The Rifle Range is probably the most boring aspect of our training because we all stand or sit around awaiting our turn to get into position and fire our weapons. Because of my experience with weapons as a child, I always qualify as an expert marksman.

All the boys in the neighborhood, whose parents can afford it, have a 22 rifle. Because of our poverty, my two brothers and I share one rifle. Dad manages to scrape up enough money to buy us a few shells every once in a while. We are told, "Use them sparingly." Boys being boys, we throw cans in the air and waste a lot of shells shooting at them, so we are out of shells most of the time. We also take turns seeing who can hit small branches and twigs by using the sight. You may be asking, "How can you sight with your right eye when you wear a patch over it." I have failed to mention that I only wear the patch when I am inactive, because I cannot see well enough to find my way around when my right eye is covered.

I do not have much luck at shooting game animals while hunting, although I try my best. One day while hunting for squirrels I spot one up in a tree and when I fire my 22 rifle, it falls. I go to pick it up but do not see it. Looking around I spot it standing in a depression in the base of the tree trunk facing the tree with it's tail sticking straight up it's back and its paws are over it's eyes as if hiding. I am so desperate to return home with a kill that I take my hunting knife and stab it in the back. When I dress it for Mom to fry I cannot find any wounds on it other than the fatal knife wound so, from then on, every time I think about it I am nauseated with the thought, "I have murdered a poor little squirrel."

Participating in hand grenade training, we have advanced to training with live grenades. There is always someone who will mess up, like the one trainee in our group who is instructed to pull the safety pin of the live grenade, release the activating lever, count to three, and then throw the grenade. He does everything just as he is instructed until he is about to make the throw, but instead of throwing it, he drops the activated grenade right in our midst. I give the sergeant who is conducting the training great accolades for his swift action in shouting, "Everybody down," and he picks up the grenade and throws it where it explodes before it ever hits the ground.

The area above the cemetery is saturated with small private coal mines and all the coal miners store their dynamite in a small shed just off from the entrance of their respective mine. None of these sheds are locked, so we have unlimited access to as many sticks of dynamite as we want. Taking my share of dynamite sticks and using my pocket knife I cut a small branch from a tree, stick it in the ground, and again using my knife I cut a stick of dynamite in half, then I tie the halves to the branch with the cut edges up. Striking a match, (we all carry a water proof container of matches in our pocket along with our pocket knife,) on the thigh of my pants I apply the flame to the dynamite, then jump back and watch as the dynamite spews sparks into the air, with much more intensity than the fourth of July sparklers.

Blasting caps and lengths of fuse are also plentiful, so we carry these items plus the dynamite and matches into the forest, until we find a large dead tree trunk lying on the ground near a depression. Inserting a blasting cap and a short length of fuse into the end of a stick of dynamite, we lay behind the log, light the fuse, wait a second, lob the stick in an over hand toss, yell, "Fire in the hole," and get our kicks when the dynamite explodes with a tremendous bang. This all sounds very dangerous, but we never have a mishap.

The physical aspect of our training is climaxed with a thirty two mile forced march. This really separates the men from the boys. We march at quick step for a while; then we go to double time, then back to quick step, then back to double time, etc., etc. etc.

I keep hearing a rifle hit the asphalt, then a helmet and we stop long enough to move the fallen man to the side of the road to be picked up by the ambulance that is bringing up the rear, then we continue our march. Hurrah, hurrah: Upon completion of this march we are now qualified for combat-almost.

The majority of the troops are given leave with orders to report for overseas deployment as regular infantrymen. Those of us held back are broken down into small groups for specialized training. I am assigned to a unit to take Anti Tank training on a 57 mm anti-tank gun. This is an artillery piece pulled by a three quarter ton weapon's carrier. The training is quite extensive as we are taught all the vulnerable spot to shoot at on a German tank in order to disable it.

We have all the components of the gun drilled into our heads, and the drill of setting up, loading and firing the gun is a break from the monotony. For the conclusion of our training, all the teams are pitted against each other to see who can get the gun set up and fired in the least amount of time. Each individual gun crew is sitting in the back of their respective weapons carrier that has an anti tank gun in tow. As we move along, a whistle is blown; the trucks come to a halt, the men unload, disengage the gun, set it up, load it and the gunner yells fire. My gun crew sets a new record in this drill; this is not a quote, and I believe it is eight seconds, flat.

CHAPTER
11

PRE DEPLOYMENT LEAVE

Our training is finally concluded on 18 December, 1944, and I am granted leave for the Christmas and New Years holidays, along with orders to report to Fort George G. Meade at its conclusion, for deployment overseas. I spend my leave at home in Johnstown, Pennsylvania and I am afraid I sort of unintentionally neglect Mom by spending so much of my daytime hours doing volunteer welding jobs for my friends and working with Dad repairing houses. I also go to a leatherworker and have him make me a harness for my hunting knife scabbard. I now can carry my pride and joy knife slung under my left arm pit, and I pack it away in my duffle bag for future use.

A few days into my leave, I go into a pizzeria in Morrellville, to buy square slices of pizza to take home. While there, this tall slender girl walks in and we are both smitten with what we think is true love. After being away from home and working at Baldwins I have now overcome my shyness so I approach her and talk to her and take her to a movie that evening. I am too rambunctious to stay at home during the evenings, so I spend most of them at my girl friends house. She suggests we get married but I tell her, "No, I am not going to go off and get killed and leave behind a widow with a kid."

⟨ COMBAT ⟩

CHAPTER
12

JOURNEY TO WAR

On 2, January 1945, when my leave is concluded, with duffle bag hanging from my right shoulder, I board a train and start the first leg of my journey to war by reporting for duty at Fort George G. Meade, Maryland. Dusk has settled in by the time all us new arrivals are taken into a barracks and ordered, "Everyone claim a bunk and place your duffle bag on it, then fall into formation in the street in front of the barracks." I am billeted in a barracks of complete strangers with nothing in writing to show any information or instructions on any of this.

When every one has placed his belongings, (many individuals are hard headed and ignore the instructions on their leave orders to arrive at camp with only a duffle bag,) on their bunks we fall out and are marched to an auditorium for processing for overseas duty. We start with what seems a never ending series of shots to guard against any bugs we might encounter in a foreign country. Then we are indoctrinated to avoid any contact with women because they are all the carriers of every disease known to man.

Out in the street everyone falls into formations to make the return trip to our barracks. Every one but me, that is. I can not recognize anyone so I do not know which formation I am supposed to be in. I stand alone as the formations move out. My brilliant mind kicks into gear. "They must be going in the general direction of my barrack," so I follow along in a one man formation. When the formations stop, I discover I have made a boo-boo. I had failed to take note of the number of the barracks where I had placed my duffle bag. Checking out one barracks after another I finally come across my duffle bag with my name stenciled on it laying on the bunk I had chosen. There is a lesson to be learned from each new boondoggle. This one teaches me that from now on I will pay extra special attention to all my surroundings. The next morning the word is announced, "Any baggage other than your duffle bag has to be disposed of. You can do this by either mailing the extra bags home, or you can place them on the sidewalk in front of the barracks, for you will leave here with only your duffle bag." It would be a story in itself, to trace the journey of all this disposed of luggage and the contents within.

With the fear of looking at anyone of the opposite sex, for the rest of our lives imbedded in our minds, we transfer to Fort Dix, New Jersey to await the arrival of a ship at the docks of New York Harbor, to transport us to an unknown area of the world; presumably Europe.

While processing at Fort Dix, I draw guard duty, and I am transported by truck, miles out from the main camp where I am posted at a motor pool for my shift, from 0200 hours to 0600 hours. I do not get relieved at 0600 so I wait at the gate next to the highway to hitch a ride back to camp. Not a solitary vehicle comes by, until approaching midday when I manage to flag down a staff car traveling in the direction of the main camp. Explaining my dilemma to the colonel who is driving the car, he has me get in the back seat and takes me back to the guard house only to find it all closed up. The guard detail has been disbanded and I have been forgotten, so I go to my barrack to await the repercussions, but none materializes. The fact that I had climbed onto the seat of a large truck and gone to sleep may have contributed to my not being relieved, but in that case another guard would have been posted, so I was just plain forgotten. I can see "I am going to be an outstanding soldier."

Three days of lying around in the barracks, eating, sleeping and filled with complete boredom elapses, when we hear the announcement over the loud speaker, "A ship has docked in New York and is ready for boarding." We are finally given a loading manifest to read, so taxing my eyes, I put my mind to work. One name I recognize on the listing is Boring Irvin L. Private First Class. Further examination reveals the names of some of my basic training buddies, but they are scattered so we have not had any encounters. We are transported by trucks to the docks in the New York harbor where we unload and take our first look at the ship on which we will be sailing. What a ship we gaze at. It is, "The Queen Mary" and as I look it over I detect no signs of any armament. We finally board the Queen, with the order to lie in our assigned fold down canvas berths until we are given the okay to get up and about. I am assigned the lower bunk with three above me. These bunk are so cramped I can lie down but there is not enough head room to sit up. After what seems forever we are given the word we can get up and about, but we are not to leave our compartment until the okay is given.

I wait and I wait, with great expectations of seeing the Statue of Liberty and finally hear the words on the ships intercom, "All troops are now free to go up on the open deck." Ascending to the open deck, all I can see in any direction is water and the horizons. We have sailed so smoothly I had not felt the ship move. This day is 8 January, 1945, and the Queen is out of the harbor on open water. I am sailing towards an unknown destination, and being aboard the Queen Mary, I presume our destination is England and I have not seen the Lady. My curiosity for exploring takes me as far as I can go to the fore and aft of the ship with me giving close scrutiny of every visible inch of the deck, and I still find no trace of any armament. I approach a British sailor and ask, "Where are all the guns?" and I am told, "There are no guns because the Queen is too fast for any bloody enemy to catch." This news give me a queasy feeling in my stomach, because I had read about the sinking of troop ships by the Germans and here we are defenseless and what I consider vulnerable.

Crowded as we are, I start bumping into others from my basic training gang so my feeling of being a stranger vanishes. The meals served on the Queen are some of the most scrumptious meals one can expect to have set before them. That is if you have a taste for fat, fat, fat, pork chops. The chops, beautifully thick, boiled in navy beans are about 70% fat, 10% bone and perhaps 20% lean. Believe me when I tell you, that as awful as the food tasted going down, it tastes much worse coming up. This foul smelling meal is served so often I believe the ship's dietician, or food suppliers, and the cooks think, "Why prepare anything decent when it is just wasted food."

The ship is large enough that when it hits a swell, there is very little up and down motion from bow to stern. On the other hand the keel is so wide there is a tremendous side to side roll. This fact and being entombed below deck, plus, the stench from the galley causes everyone nausea. The aroma of concoctions cooking engulfs the entire ship, so by the time the first spoonful is dished out, a great percentage of the troops are so seasick they can not get out of their berth even to vomit so they up chuck right in their beds. The deck stays slimy and ungodly stinky from all this up chucking, making the job of cleaning it up just that much more unpleasant for those of us still mobile enough to continuously mop it up.

I am on the open deck staring at the horizon to keep my stomach from churning. "I had thrown up as much as the next guy but found out how to control it." I compare my stomach to the bubble in a level, no matter how much the ends of the level move up and down, the bubble in the level stays horizontal. Affixing my gaze on the horizon stops the swishing motion in my stomach. The odor on the open deck is about the same as it is below deck because a lot of the troops who share my idea of controlling their stomachs have the misfortune of puking into the wind.

Three days at sea, the ships loudspeakers are entertaining the troops with what appears to be Britans favorite terrible taste in radio programs, (some sort of quiz show), when things are interrupted with an announcement, this is not an exact quote, "Attention, attention all ships at sea, be on the lookout for survivors, for we have just been informed the Queen Mary has been sunk, with all hands on board." It is quit a shock at first, standing there being told we have all drowned. The humor of it sets in when we realize the announcement is just propaganda to confuse the enemy.

We make port at Glasgow, Scotland, on 14 January, 1945, six days from setting sail. The Queen is too large to be tied up at the docks, so it anchors about five hundred yards out in the bay. We descend deck after deck from the main deck and transfer to a smaller, but still a large ship, to make dock. Disembarking at the dock, we shoulder our duffle bags and climb all those wooden steps.

Stepping off the top step, we walk a couple of hundred yards to a waiting train, and as soon as all the troops have boarded, we depart on our journey south. It is early evening and still light when we pull out, starting our trip, passing through fields saturated with large holes that appear as bomb craters and everything is a lush green. Night sets in and so do we for the long trip south. Before long the train is engulfed in a light fog that gets denser by the hour. In the wee hours of the morning it is announced, "We are now passing through London" but there is nothing to see because looking out the window there is nothing but a wall of fog that makes me wonder, "How can the engineer travel at such a high speed when the visibility is zero?"

Upon arrival at the docks of Southampton in mid morning, we transfer to smaller ships, and as soon as all the troops are aboard, we set sail. As we sail across the lower end of the English Channel, we pass a mass of scattered amphibians, sunk during the sea invasion of the beaches of France. Tied up at the dock in the port of LaHarve, France, it is in the darkness of evening by the time we are all assembled on the dock, where we stand around for hours. Finally we load onto a train and travel the night to a replacement depot, located somewhere in France. While awaiting further deployment I figure it is time to strap on my hunting knife with it's sheath tucked under my left armpit. The gadget feels awkward for a while, and I continuously practice reaching across my chest with my right hand, unsnapping the snap on the knife sheath flap, and drawing the knife until the action comes naturally. As time elapses I no longer am aware I have it on. It is a part of me.

The morning of 21 January, 1945 we are informed we are moving up to join the fighting units located at various locations on the front battle lines. We are marched to a string of six boxcars, "forty & eights," (each boxcar will hold forty men or eight mules), sitting on the tracks of a railroad switch yard and we are loaded into them.

The first soldier gently places his rifle on the floor, throws his duffle bag through the open, sliding, side door, climbs in, retrieves his gear and moves to the front left corner of the car. He places his duffle bag against the wall in this far corner of the boxcar. His rifle is leaned against the bag, his back pack is removed and placed on top of his duffle bag, and then he places himself with his feet against the duffle bag and stands facing the front wall. The next soldier places his gear next to the first duffle bag and takes his standing position facing his gear. This routine is carried out until the row extends, from the left side wall to the right side wall. The same scenario is carried out with each row, with a slight variation from the first row. The second and the succeeding rows have the duffle bags placed up against the soldiers feet in the preceding row, and the last space in the row is left vacant, leaving a corridor for unloading and reloading, and this routine is carried out until the floor is covered from wall to wall leaving the one vacant space at the end of each row on the door side of the car. We are jammed so close we cannot move, let alone sit or stretch.

The walls of the boxcar are solid except for a few open slots along the top of the side walls for ventilation, too high to look through and when the door is slid shut we are in almost darkness and our knees are hurting before the train even starts on its way. Every four hours the train stops, the troops unload to stretch and relieve themselves, then back to the sardine can, leaving behind who knows what kind of odors?

CHAPTER
13

INITIATION TO COMBAT

Night sets in and time drags; some soldiers in the boxcar are wearing luminous dial watches and someone is always asking, "What time is it?"

The owner of one of theses watches replies, "1805"

After what seems a long time another soldier asks, "What time is it now?"

"You just asked me that five minutes ago. It's 1810."

Things are quiet for a while and the question is asked again.

"It's three minutes since you asked me that; it's now 1813."

The questions and answers go on and on. Just after the last answer of, "It's 2015 hours," someone remarks, "I think I heard gun fire," and the train stops, backs up, then comes to another stop. The door is opened, we unload and a sergeant informs us, "As the train started through the pass the engine came under fire from a machine gun up on the hill on the right of the train, so the engineer backed out of danger, I need ten volunteers to go silence the machine gun."

Hostilities have been declared over in Northern France, so we are to encounter no enemy troops, therefore there is no need for ammunition. We have not been issued any shells for our rifles. I commit a no-no by volunteering. The sergeant has the ten of us crawl back into the car and get our cartridge belts and our rifles. I do not know where they have it stored, but by the time we emerge from the car the sergeant produces and passes five clips of ammo to each volunteer. Loading a clip into our rifles and putting the other four clips into our cartridge belts and led by the sergeant, the eleven of us go back into the pass, staying as close to the hill as possible. It is dark and an extra-ordinarily clear evening, so visibility is quite good. The machine gun gives a burst of fire at us and we all hit the dirt. The sergeant orders, "Spread out and move towards the gun, firing as you go." In the darkness it is so hard to make out anything it is a miracle none of us greenhorns shoot one another and by the time we reach the gunner's spot up on the hill at the tree line, the gunner and gun are gone.

Back at the train we turn in the ammunition we have left and it is now 0200 hours of 22, January 1945 by the time we are all loaded back into the cars and proceed on our merry way. I have just had the displeasure of experiencing my first exposure to enemy fire. The train makes one more pit stop just as day breaks then travels continuously until 1100 hours and stops at a station in a small town. The troops unload and we are broken up into small groups that load onto various means of transportation, to be taken to our assigned units. Myself and three of my basic training buddies are dropped off of the three quarter ton truck in a small village. I believe it is in Northern France. Carrying our gear we are escorted into a building and hear, "Boy are we glad to see you guys; go across the street and look in the garage."

Leading the way across the dirt street to the large roll away garage door, I open it's built in, small entrance door and start to step through. I pull my foot back when I see a pile of dead American soldiers, stacked one on top of the other, like cordwood with their head next to the door and their feet towards the center of the garage. The bodies are lying on their backs; the top one having his head tilted back to extremes, his wide open eyes seeming to stare right at me. This sight creates a tremendous shock or jolt to my system and when I step back and the other three in turn take their look, each one turns away and vomits.

All of the combat hardened troops who have followed us to the garage are standing behind us in the street watching our reactions. They break out in laughter at this spectacle. The four of us see nothing at all funny or humorous about this stack of dead soldiers and the shock it gives to our system. Here is the first indication that I am just a bit above the rest of us replacements, for I keep my innards under control and do not upchuck. The reason I am able to cope with the situation is because I had this strange quirk as a child of coming across dead bodies, so I had encountered death on many occasions during my growing years.

Walking to Edgewood Elementary School in the morning, we cross a one lane wooden bridge over St. Clair Run, then travel a path leading away from the stream and along the side of a hill. We hit a paved road and again pass close to St. Clair Run before getting to school. While every one else follows the path, I climb down under the bridge, follow the stream or creek by jumping from stone to stone and what dry ground I can find along the bank. Arriving at the point where the creek comes close to the road I ascend the steep bank and pick up the regular route to school. The other kids arrive at school ahead of me, and I am usually tardy and wet during the warm days and wet and cold on winter days from falling though the ice into the shallow water. For these escapades I receive detention after the school day ends, but this does not stop me from doing the same thing over and over again; at least I am persistent and consistent in my shenanigans.

This morning I take the creek route, and where I usually climb up the bank, I spot a large rock in the water that I have never noticed before. Wondering how it got there, I take a close look and it is not a rock at all; it is the body of a dead man laying face down in the water, bloated and swollen to a huge, gross proportion. When I get to school I tell my teacher, "There's a dead man down in St. Clair Run at Nash Street." She does not believe me, but I persist with my story so she sends me to the principal's office to tell my tale to the principal. Anyone reporting to the principal's office does so in fear of the large wooden paddle with all the holes drilled in it. If I am caught in a lie my bottom will be mighty sore when I leave the principles office. I repeat my story to the principal' who says, "I will have someone check out your

*story," and I am sent back to class. I check on the way home
from school and the body is gone.*

*Since we are discussing St. Clair Run I want to bring up
the subject of bootlegging. The selling of alcoholic beverages
is forbidden by law, so pubs, saloons and night clubs cannot
legally buy and sell alcohol. They remain open, but no
alcoholic drinks are allowed, and because people are going
to drink booze, a lot of bootleggers set up stills in their
homes. For some strange reason the government revenuers
just cannot seem to locate these still to put the bootleggers
out of business. The byproduct or waste produced by stills,
is a white foam given off of the cooking of corn and mash.
Every little itty bitty tributary emptying into St. Clair Run,
runs thick with this white foam, and I, being a mere child
could follow the foam right to the house of its origin, but
for some strange reason the revenuers cannot figure this out.
Does this imply something is being done to make bootlegging
a lucrative business. If, for some reason, a bootlegger gets
in disfavor with a revenuer, you can get drunk from the
alcoholic fume emitted from the cement drainage culverts
where the revenuers use their axes to break open the white
lightning containers and dump the contents. Let's move on.*

*Letting the time slip by and overstaying our time in the
forest, it has turned dark and knowing our parents will
be worrying about us, Jerry, two years my senior and I are
running down a steep path through the cemetery. Jerry has a
good lead on me, so when I trip and fall over legs sticking out
into the path, I get up and ask, "What's the matter Jerry, did
you fall?" From away down the path, Jerry shouts, "What
did you say?" I get real scared and run down to where he is*

waiting and tell him, "I tripped over a man's legs and I think he is dead." We run the one block to my house and tell Dad, "There's a dead man laying in the path in the graveyard." He sends Jerry to bring back his dad. The four of us take my lantern and return to the spot where I tripped, and sure enough, the body is lying there.

After spending the day alone in the forest, scavenging fruits and berries, it has become dark, so in my haste to get home I am running along the electric power poles that stand in the center of the cleared right of way that carries electricity up the hill to the two city water tanks. As I am passing a power pole, I am struck a terrible blow to my forehead, causing my feet to run out from under me, flipping me to the ground on my back. Picking myself up I look to see what has hit me. A body is dangling from the end of a rope, scaring me to the point that I take off running towards Morrellville. I stop a man on Fairfield Avenue and tell him what happened.

He of course, does not believe me and escorts me home. Entering the house I exclaim excitedly; "Mom, Dad; I was just knocked down by a dead man hanging from the cross beam of an electricity line pole." Dad, the man and I carry my lantern to the pole and they can not believe what they are seeing. The man leaves to get the police and while we await his return Dad and I look the scene over. We try figuring how the man managed to get the rope over the cross beam, tie the end to the pole, put the noose around his neck and hang himself. There are no climbing spikes in the pole and there is nothing he could have stood on, then kicked it out from under himself. One look by our great police and one makes the statement, "It looks like suicide to me," and the other one nods his head in agreement. It is officially ruled a suicide, but Dad and I do not agree with this statement.

I owe that dead man, or the true culprit or culprits a word of thanks, because instead of the leather belt for being so late, the only punishment I receive from Dad is, "Let this be a lesson to you about staying in the woods so late. Now maybe you'll get come home before dark."

A man who lives up the hill from us has a small coal mine in the forest above the cemetery, where he extracts a little coal for his own private use. One day he fails to return home from the mine so his wife alerts the men of the neighborhood that he had gone to the mine and has not returned. I am just seven years old, but Dad and three other men take me with them to the mine, making me the only child present. Dad works part time in various mines so he wears his miner' cap with its carbide lamp. He often lets me accompany him into the mines, so I wear the little hat with its lamp that Mom has made for me. The entrance to this little mine is no more than three feet high and sort of round. A man calls into the mine but gets no response so they all talk it over and decide the mine is too small to permit any of them to properly maneuver in it.

One man looks at me and says, "Lee, light your lamp and be a brave little boy and go in and see if he's there. Don't be scared." I am small enough that I am able to crawl on my hands and knees with ease. About thirty feet in I see the soles of the man's shoes and the toes are pointing down.

"He's here. I see his feet," I yell.

Someone calls in, "See if you can move them. Don't be afraid."

I swallow the fear of touching a dead man, but with my right hand I grab ahold of the heel of his right foot, move it back and forth and the foot moves. "I can move them," I shout.

"Okay. Come out."

Out of the mine the man asks me, "Just what did you see?"

"He's lying on his stomach. I saw his feet but nothing happened when I shook them."

Someone shouts; "Go fetch a long rope," and one of the men takes off at a run.

"Boy," The man says, "Now pay attention. He might be dead so he can't hurt you. Grit your teeth and go back in there and see if any rocks have fallen on him."

Back inside I am scared to death but I steel myself, move up as close as I can, even stretching over his legs and call back, "I can't see anything on him."

"Alright come back out." The man says.

The men stand there fidgeting not saying much and pretty soon the rope arrives. A loop is made on one end of it with a slip knot and I am instructed, "You're doing real good boy, now listen careful again. Go in and put his feet together. Then slip the loop around his ankles and pull the loop tight."

"Yes sir," and I do as instructed, give the word that I am done, and then watch as the men pull. It works. The man is moving. Someone calls in to me, "Stay by his feet and back out as we pull and make sure his feet don't get caught on anything." I move backwards as instructed. At the time I do not know if he is alive or dead and we are out with no hang-ups.

A huge piece of slate or stone had fallen from the roof just grazing the top of his head, peeling his scalp off his skull, which is a shiny white. The scalp is hanging loose and when they turn him over it covers his eyes, and his nose is all torn up from the dragging. He is alive but unconscious so they put his scalp back into place, send someone to bring a blanket and when the blanket arrives he is placed in it and carried home. I do not know when the man regains consciousness but miraculously in time the scalp adheres to his skull and he survives.

A mass murder has taken place in a log cabin in the foothills of the other side of Laurel Mountain about twelve miles from our house, by way of the highway. Dad takes me to the scene. He doesn't take my two brothers with us because this is too delicate for them to see. The only means of transportation we have is our feet so we take a short cut through the cemetery, follow Mountain Road up Laurel Mountain and pass under the sagging great length of wire between the power line steel towers that run along the crest of the mountain. This time, as with the other times I have passed under the wires I experience the exposure to large amounts of static electricity and my hair tingles so much I think it is standing straight up. Dad explains to me, "If you are ever caught up here in a rainstorm, never pass under the wires or climb one of the towers. The electricity might jump from the wire to the tower and kill you."

I cannot pass by any climbable structure without climbing it. The conventional way to ascend to the observation room at the top of the forest rangers fire observation tower on Laurel Mountain is to ascend the stairs from landing to landing. To get to this room on top of the steel framed tower, Dad and everyone else but me uses the stairs; I climb the steel frame up to the last landing then moved to the center and enter the observation room through the trap door in the center of the floor. Dad is scared to death I will fall but he tolerates any unorthodox method I have of doing things. He is letting me develop my skills.

Passing any light poles, they seem to beckon, "Come Lee, climb me." Some poles have climbing spikes that start about eight feet from the ground so I use my climbing ability to the first spike, then up the pole I go. Some poles have no spikes so I shimmy up the pole to where the guy wires are connected to the pole. I transfer to one and, hanging under the guy wire, I shimmy to the ground. Every steel cable has a broken strand or two so I arrive at school or any other destination with bleeding hands.

Once we have passed under the power line and start our decent down the other side of Laurel Mountain the road turns into a path of over growth and trees. As we near the foothills it again becomes a passable road that brings us to where it intersects with the Haws Pike. Here we turn right, follow along the highway then make another right that takes us up a dirt road to the cabin.

The cabin has all the inside walls and floors covered with mattresses. The mattresses on the floors, the walls and even ceiling with no mattress, as well as the front porch are all splattered with blood. Though I am only about seven, Dad explains to me, "This is a place where grown ups come and hold sex parties." Of course I am too young to comprehend what he is telling me. When our observation of the cabin is completed, we retrace our route back home.

At trial it is established that three couples were having a fling, when something went wrong and all were shot, except the one male survivor who is a prominent doctor in Johnstown. At trial, the judge believed the doctors claims, that one man had killed the four, and he had to kill the man in self defense, so the judge lets him off free as a bird.

These dead soldiers lying in the garage are members of the 1st Platoon, "B" Company, 101 Infantry Regiment, 26 Infantry Division, of the Massachusetts National Guard who had been killed the previous day. The four of us newly arrivals are their replacements. I never think to pose the question, "Where are we?" I believe the Amy is a cesspool of waste, because after all the time and effort, and the monetary expenditure to provide me with specialized training I end up being a plain infantryman.

The morning after joining the outfit we leave the village with the bodies still lying in the garage, and join up with the rest of "B" company in a large field to await orders as to where we will go next. Lolling around with nothing to do, curiosity gets the better of me so I go exploring the countryside. As I step out into a field an unusual mound of branches and leaves catches my attention. I get the premonition something is unusual about this pile and my curiosity is aroused. The removal of several branches exposes a sloping, large wooden door, just like the outside basement doors in farm houses in the states. I clear away enough area exposing the whole door and open the door.

I cannot believe such a long set of wooden stairs, with hand rails, going deep into the bowels of the earth, so I carefully make my way to the bottom of these steps, and with the bit of light from the open door, I find myself in a huge wine cave with rack after rack of full wine bottles. Finding a very large burlap sack lying on the dirt floor I pick it up and fill it with as many bottles as I can carry, and return to the real world. I think, "How could the Germans have overlooked such a simple camouflage?" I close the door, put back the branches and leaves as best I can, and leave with the sack slung over my right shoulder. I do not drink wine, but I am taking it back for my fellow troops.

As I approach the field where my fellow troops are staying, I encounter a pathetic looking soldier who asks, "What do you have in the sack?"

I tell him, "It's full of wine."

He orders, "Take it back to where you got it."

I remark, "Who the hell are you to order me around?"

"I'm Lieutenant _ _ _ _ _of the second platoon; and I'm giving you a direct order to get rid of it, so move it."

"Oh," I exclaim, shoulder the sack, carry it until I am out of the Lt's sight, place it under a tree and return to my platoon. I wonder who had the good fortune to discover that sack full of perfectly good wine.

In mid afternoon we move out in freezing weather and pass body after body of frozen enemy troops and animals, plus untold numbers of disabled vehicles of both the German and United States Armies. As I sit on the frozen carcass of a horse and consume a can of rations the reality suddenly sets in that we are not in a game, but that we are in a war and in a couple of hours our feet transport us into the already cleared city of Wiltz, Luxembourg. Having read and heard about the, "Battle of the Bulge," I know Wilts is in Luxembourg so I realize I had made an error the day before when I assumed we were in northern France.

Taking shelter in an empty tavern, we sit or lay around on the floor all night. The next morning when we hear a German 88 artillery shell pass overhead, a battle hardened technical sergeant who is a big man, "not fat, just a huge man," makes a dive and goes down the basement stairs almost head first. A track star could not have moved any faster and several of us greenhorns follow suit.

Waiting out the shelling, the sergeant explains, "If you hear an 88 shell you don't have to worry because it has already passed."

I ask, "If that's true why did you make such a dive down the stairs?"

He then tells us about the pattern of the 88 used by the German artillery and tanks, "The first shell is over shot, the second one is short and the third one hits dead center." Being a greenhorn I take in his every word.

Being a novice at combat, I have lots and lots to learn, and as we are advancing across a field I hear this ear piercing, screaming eerie sound from overhead that causes me to ball my fists and my body to tremble. Turning my head and looking to my left I see a group of small explosions in the dirt among the shrubs on the side of a low rise some distance from the edge of the field. It is mid winter and the only damage I can see is small fires among these bushes. I yell to a nearby soldier who is a hardened combatant, "What the hell was that?"

He shouts back, "Not that, but those. They are screaming meemies and are supposed to shatter our nerves as they pass overhead."

"Well they sure do a good job of it because I'm still shaking."

As we continue on our way I wonder, "Were those shells fired with the intent of hitting us in the field and the distance miscalculated, or were they fired long intentionally for the sole purpose of playing on our minds?"

It takes only a few days of being addressed as "Mister Lee," by my three buddies until the other troops of the platoon pick it up.

Advancing through a city in Luxembourg clearing buildings and being a greenhorn, I make the mistake of ignoring the buddy system, and go off on my own to a building on my left. Opening the large front door, I pass through what seems to be a lobby to the next door and opening it, I am looking at a long room with three bowling alleys on the left and a huge empty space on the right. I am in a bowling alley. As I move through the empty space a door in the right wall eases open a bit and a German soldier starts to come through the doorway. This is my first contact and sighting of a German soldier and we are both startled. Seeing me, he jumps back and lets the door go shut. I station myself facing the door calling out several times in German, "Comrade, come here." When the door fails to open, the several shots I fire through the wall convinces him to come out. The door eases open and the soldier appears in the doorway with his hands in the air over his head, and he is shaking with fear, like a leaf fluttering on a tree. He is young.: I am just eighteen and know I have several years on this kid. He has no weapon and has probably stayed behind when his outfit evacuated the city so he could be taken prisoner.

The other troops hear the shooting, so they come investigating and when the combat hardened troops see my prisoner, I really get a good chastising and am informed, "We never take prisoners, so you should have killed the little bastard." My platoon leader says to me, "This is your goof so you will have to guard him until someone takes him back to the rear. Do not make this mistake again."

My platoon assembles in the bowling ally, where we spread out on the floor and spend the night, and I believe I get less sleep that night than the prisoner. The next morning a staff sergeant volunteers to take the prisoner to the rear echelon area, and turn him over to headquarters as prisoner of war. About twenty minutes after their departure the sergeant returns and tells everyone, "That damn little Kraut bastard tried to escape and I had to shoot him." On hearing these spoken words, it takes only an instant for me to mature several years. Everyone slaps the Sgt. on the back, laughs and comments, "You sure took care of that Kraut." That is; everyone laughs but me.

What a terrible mistake in judgment the young German soldier had made. Capturing him is the cruelest act I can possibly have committed. Had I shot him on sight he would have died an honorable death. Why would a man go through such an ordeal to get captured and then attempt an escape?

Later in the day I am standing guard duty in the doorway of the bowing ally, with the door shut, when an 88 artillery shell hits the church steeple directly across the street from the doorway in which I am standing. The blast shatters the steeple, causing wood chips and shrapnel to pepper the door frame all around me. The other troops come out to see what the explosion is all about, and cannot believe I do not have a scratch on me because the door and frame are all pock marked. I do not know why, but there is just the one round instead of the pattern I described earlier.

After trekking all day, we take shelter for the night in a small village somewhere in Luxembourg and I am standing guard duty in the middle of the town square. It is bitter cold and the wind is cutting right through my clothing, so in my attempt to break the wind and relieve my shivering, I am standing as close to the town stocks, located in the center of the town square, as I can get. The night is pitch black with not a glimmer or a speck of light showing anywhere, for the town must be in a blackout mode. A door opens in the corner building of the closest intersection and the darkness is pierced with a very bright beam of light. A woman carrying something steaming in her hand comes through the doorway, closes the door and I watch her as she approaches me. Neither of us speaks as her extended hands present me with a cup and saucer. Taking a sip from the cup I find it to be a hot toddy of tea and Schnapps. That angel stands there shivering with me as I sip from the cup until the contents are all consumed, then I hand the cup and saucer back to her, and I give her a big hug and say, "Thank you." She does not utter a word, just flashes a beautiful, meek smile, then turns around and retraces her steps back to the building. There is another beam of light, then the door closes and I am once again engulfed in darkness. Her offering really warms me for a few minutes, then I resume my shivering.

The bitter cold days come and go as we pass through one village or town after another, and it is a long trek, passing a never ending count of morbid scenes. Finally a truck arrives and we load up and are transported into the city of Saarlautern, Germany, as occupiers, relieving the troops who had driven the enemy out for the second time. The city is referred to as "The Dead City," because, of all the devastation caused by all the fighting that had occurred. First the Allies pushed the enemy out, only to have the Germans, return the favor with the implementation of the bulge offensive and as the bulge was coming to a conclusion, the Allies once again, reclaimed the city. All this fighting, back and fourth caused the cities inhabitants to evacuate the city and I do not encounter one during our stay in the city.

My squad takes shelter in a basement with an open stairway on the west side of a two story, wooden building. From the head of these stairs there is a one story creamery consisting of a corridor about ten feet wide and thirty feet long, with three rooms on each side of this corridor. Each room has a solid steel door, about one quarter of an inch thick and about four feet wide that opens out into the roofless corridor. All the walls, of the creamery are constructed of fieldstone, approximately eighteen inches thick. An almost flat field extends from the western outer wall of the creamery, quite a distance to a railroad embankment that runs south and north with the creamery wall.

I am standing guard duty in the last room on the right from the basement, looking to the west through a shell hole in the wall at eye level, when I hear an 88 round swish just a few feet directly over me. It explodes on the building above the basement to my rear. The second 88 round explodes about a hundred yards in front of me and my blood just seems to boil. As I recall the spoken words of the Sergeant back in Wilts I think, "Oh my god, I'm a dead man, I have to get out of here fast."

Dashing from the room as fast as I can and slamming the door shut, I just get into the room across the corridor without taking time to close the door, when this terrible explosion occurs from the direction of the basement. I know the shell has gone down the basement stairs and wiped out my squad. When the dust clears and I regain my senses, I see the third 88 round had passed through the wall under the hole I had been looking through, deflected slightly, and its momentum carried it through the steel door to the head of the basement stairs. It exploded on the cement landing about eighteen inches short of the stairs. Had I remained at my lookout the shell would have passed right through my chest, "Thank you, Sergeant!"

This is an assumption on my part: Bypassed German units have been attempting to get back to Germany, but we are in their way. A tank and its crew must have been stranded and are trying to get back to there own lines, and in so doing, they posted a lookout or observer with binoculars on the railroad embankment. It is early evening and with the sun shining through the hole, I must have been illuminated like a picture in an art gallery. My image in his binoculars must have given him to assume there are other troops in the building in my immediate area, and so he decides to shell us. I can just imagine the exuberating expression on his face, when he got the dead center hit, thinking he has taken care of that lousy Yankee and his buddies.

Later in the night, around 0200 hours, I am again standing guard duty, looking west through another small shell hole at eye level in a little room on the side of the creamery, just across from the basement stairs. The night is pitch dark and absolutely quiet when, without warning. an object appears in the hole not more than a foot from my eyes. Although I am startled, instinct makes me utter, "Hiss," startling the black cat so bad, it omits a shrill of a scream and does a back flip out of the hole. My entire squad comes rushing out of the basement to find out what caused such a terrible scream.

CHAPTER
14

HOW I BECOME A SCOUT
AND LEAD MAN

Relieved of our occupational duties and trucked from Saarlautern, we are dropped off at an unknown location and start our trek across Germany, engaging the enemy, anywhere the upper echelon figures we are needed. It is late evening as my platoon settles down to spend the night in a building of a small town we have cleared. The building we are in is located in the center of town and consists of four concrete walls, with all the windows broken out, the roof is missing, the concrete floor is covered with a scattering of straw, and it is too cold to lay down and sleep.

At 2300 hours one of my greenhorn buddies who does not know he is volunteering to do an act requiring great courage answers the platoon leader's request for a volunteer to accompany a battle hardened staff sergeant to check out the area between us and the next town we are to clear in the morning. After the patrol has left we spend the night awaiting their return, by sitting, standing, pacing and beating our bodies in our attempt at keeping warm. Hours pass, with the continuous shivering persisting someone commits a no-no and lights a sprig of straw with his lighter. He spends the rest of the night burning one sprig of straw after the other until about 0500, and it is amazing the false feeling of heat this one little flame creates.

First Lieutenant Evans who is holding both positions as company commander and first platoon leader, asks for two volunteers to go look for the two scouts that have not returned by the designated time. I again break the rule of, "Never Volunteer;" by standing and make my speech, "All these other men have wives and loved ones to think about. If I get killed my mom will cry, my dad will be proud of me, my brothers and my sister will say that's too bad, and my girl friend will find someone else, so I'll go alone."

Lt. Evans tells me, "It is policy to use the buddy system when on patrol, but if you insist, move out."

I had paid little attention to the instructions the scouting pair had received, so I ask, "What direction should I take?"

"You know as much about that as I do. They headed in the direction of the next town. Just follow the dirt road."

There is only one dirt road leading out of town so in the dawning light I follow it, and about a quarter of a mile out I find my private first class basic training buddy, lying on his back on the right side of the road. He is in shock and delirious, from his shattered upper left arm and his shattered left thigh. He does not recognize me, grabs me with his right hand and keeps repeating over and over,

101

"Sniper, sniper, sniper!" I am making all the efforts I can to stop the bleeding, to no avail, when the platoon, led by Lt. Evans, shows up and he tells me, "We could not wait any long and had to move out. Leave him for the medic to take care of and move out." I continue along the road with a high embankment to my left and after traveling a couple of hundred yards I see the back of the sergeant, laying very still at the top of the embankment as if he is making an observation over the top of the bank.

Making my way up the bank to him, I see a jagged hole in the back of his helmet. Upon closer inspection I discover he has been shot right between his eyes and the bullet had passed through his head leaving the hole in the back of his helmet. The troops approach, the platoon leader comes up the bank, confirms the sergeant is dead and orders, "Mister Lee, move out." I am now the company's "lead man or point." Feeling a large lump in my throat that I believe is my heart, I do as I am instructed, as I did when I was a child. I take a big gulp to settle my heart and go over the bank expecting a bullet any moment. Crossing the field to a clump of trees in the middle of the field I can see the town we are to clear, so as I motion the troops to join me I fail to recognize things are going too easy.

The other troops join me, also not suspecting we are being set up. When they are all with me in the trees, two burp guns open up from the two corners of the field next to the town. Lucky for us the snow in the patch of trees is about a foot deep from the sun not being able to penetrate and melt it. I am laying just to the right of Lt. Evans and I have snow up both of my sleeves and under the collar of my cumbersome overcoat, but despite the cold I am still sweating.

The forward observer for the field artillery who is with us, uses our field phone to contact his unit to open up on the gun positions with mortars, and this Lieutenant really had trained well for his job. Just a short while after the lieutenant gives his coordinates a mortar shell lands at what we believe is a direct hit on the gun to our left front. The second one comes in, and I swear the trees sway as it passes over us to the approximate position of the second gun. Two more mortar shells hit at both gun locations and the lieutenant calls in, "Direct hits!" When the dust clears, the guns fire again so four more mortar rounds are ordered and get the same results as the first rounds. The guns are not using tracers so we can not pin point the positions to fire back. We lay there all day until it gets dark, and the guns have remained silent for a period of time when Lt. calls out, "Mister Lee."

"Yes sir I'm right here."

Lt. Evans explains to me, "If we stay here much longer we will freeze to death. Get into town and clear a building for us to move into. When you get one cleared signal us with three flashes from your flashlight."

Slithering on my stomach the two hundred or so yards to the edge of the town without drawing fire, I go between two buildings, make a left and open a door. Nothing happens so I unhook my flashlight and shine it in a sweep of the first floor of the barn. Entering, I climb the ladder to the loft, slide the large entrance door facing the field open a bit and look the field over. The night being bright and clear, I make out where the guns had been, but are now gone. I signal with my flashlight for the troops to move in, and keep repeating the flashes until I make out movement.

When all of the members of the platoon are assembled in the barn, a check is made and although reports of being hit with flying tree bark chips are made, no one is injured. I am told by Lt. Evans, "We have to clear enough of the town to get a decent building to bed down for the night." Here I go again, with my rifle at the ready, along the right edge of the paved street that begins at the barn entrance. Traveling the length of the one block street to where it junctions with a cross street, I take notice of a large church directly across the junction. The church has row houses on either side. I have traversed a paved street that is the stem of a "T."

Nearing the corner I admire the church's large stained glass window to the right of the cement steps leading up to the entranceway. Turning right at the corner I take just a few steps, when I hear a machine gun outburst. Jerking around I see glass flying and the church's beautiful window is gone. Dashing across the street I attempt to get around the church but find no openings between the buildings. Awkwardly holding my rifle I reach across my chest with my right hand, snatch the grenade from my left bandoleer sling, activate it as I move to the window opening and toss it through. As soon as the grenade explodes I crawl in, and find the gun and gunner gone, just that fast.

I think, "Surely that gun blast has gotten Lt. Evans, who is leading his troops." It is so dark I also say to myself, "I got in here so fast I hope my own men do not open fire on me." Miraculously, as I crawl out through the window Lt. Evans appears with his men close behind him. No one has had time to evaluate the casualty situation and Lt. Evans has me continue down the street, where I come to a long building on the right side of the street. After I make a sweep of it and declare it clear, it is decided it will do for the night, so we go back, gather our dead and lay them along one side of the courtyard behind the building.

As everyone is settling down on the floor for the night, I hear, "Mister Lee," and when I approach Lt. Evans, he explains to me, "There is so much artillery fire going on, from both sides, it is making me nervous and I think the Krauts might attempt to drive us back out of town. I expect some kind of action tonight by the Krauts, so to counter any such move, go back past the church, out of town as far as you think is safe. Move around during the night, and if you see any activity by the Krauts, beeline it back with the warning."

Leaving town, I travel about a half mile and decide I have come far enough, so I just stay put. As always, when I am idle, I think, "I had walked right up to the muzzle of the machine gun, and been allowed to pass, exposing, the main force to its fire. I should have known everything was going too smoothly, but how could I have imagined the Germans would stoop so low." Consoling myself with the fact, "I had no way of knowing the Germans would denigrate themselves to the level, of desecrating such a holy sanctuary, with a machine capable of such carnage." I also think, "I am no better than the Krauts because I threw that grenade into a church."

I feel terrible for letting my buddies down, by not doing my job of drawing fire on myself, thus preventing the ambush that got so many killed from that one burst of fire. I have been duped by the enemy for the second time in one day; what a terrible record I am setting for my first day as, "Lead man."

The sky stays lit up with the flashes of both German and American artillery pieces, followed by the explosion made by the respective artillery piece as they are fired, then I hear the swooshing sound as the projectiles pass overhead. The situation causes a terrible strain on my nerves to the point that after a period of time it gets to me, giving me the jitters and I start hallucinating; in my mind all the bushes and shrubs begin moving around. I remain there without incident until the pre dawn, then I returned to the town and my unit. Were I a Kraut, I could have a field day, as I walk right into town and enter the building where everyone is billeted, without even encountering one challenge.

I do not even get to lay down for some much needed sleep when Lt. Evans wants the platoon sergeant to conduct a roll call. The sergeant is nowhere to be found so the Lieutenant calls the roll himself, with all but one accounted for. He then orders me, "Go locate the sergeant." I do not know why he picks me for the task, but my actions the previous day may be playing a part in giving him confidence in me. I have no idea where to start looking, until someone says, "I heard a shot during the night from across the street."

I start my search to locate the sergeant by going across the street to an empty lot, in the still hostile section of town. Passing on the left of a German tank sitting in the center of this lot, I can see no damage to it and do not understand why it is abandoned. I turn right and as I approach the far end of the tank I see the body of the sergeant. He is about halfway between, perhaps a twenty foot space, between the tank and a building. He is on his knees, with his head on the ground, facing the building. He is still gripping his rifle and hadn't even fallen over when he got shot. The bullet entered his left shoulder, passed completely through his torso and exited the left cheek of his buttocks. The way I figure it, instead of making a dash for the building, the sergeant had gotten down and started to crawl the distance, making himself cold turkey for the German soldier and his weapon. I lay my rifle down, pry his from his grip and pick him up in a dead-man's-carry, retrieve the weapons, carry the sergeant's body to our area and place him in line with the other dead.

I think, "I should be the one dead, for had I not been in, "No-Man's-Land," and the sergeant had reason to investigate anything in the still to be cleared section of town he probably would have sent me because that is now my job. At the least he should have told someone where he was going and why. Visualize in your mind, if you can, the courage it took for the sergeant to go alone, into enemy territory in the middle of the night.

It is mid morning when our mess truck shows up, and sets up in the courtyard to prepare us our first hot meal in God only knows how many days. I am not about to miss out on food, so fighting my fatigue and sleepiness, I remain awake until the meal is dished out, and I will never forget gorging myself with meatballs and spaghetti. I sit next to my dead buddies as I eat, then I go into the first heated building I have entered in a month or so. The heat and the fatigue from no sleep for so many days catches up with me, causing so much nausea, I rush outside and lose all that good hot food, then I catch a couple of hours sleep.

Awakened at 1500 hours I am informed with the great news, "Come on, you're on guard duty." I had lost all my lunch so my stomach is growling and upon being informed by someone that the mess truck crew had replenished our C-rations, I fill my gas mask pouch with my share. Posted a couple of hundred yards beyond the fore mentioned church, I am standing just off the edge of the road under the wooden lean-to roof that provides some protection for the doorway of a small building on the right side of the dirt road. I start my stint on guard by passing a little time consuming a can of cold ham and lima beans while leaning against the door. I am still leaning against the door of the building when a jeep comes barreling down the street from the section of town we occupy. I do not know where the driver thinks he is going, and just as I step out to challenge him, there is an explosion that with the force of the blast and my own reaction knocks me back against the door. I see the front of the jeep rise into the air, then settled back down. Going to the jeep I see it has hit a mine with the passenger side front wheel, and the lieutenant riding in the passenger seat has taken the brunt of the blast with his legs.

The troops upon hearing the blast come running to see what has happened and take over. Checking my watch I see it is 1640 hours and I return to my post in the doorway. I stand and watch as the lieutenant, with his terribly mangled legs, is removed from the jeep and laid by the side of the road where our medical aid man does what he can. The lieutenant is covered with fetched blankets taken from several back packs, to keep him warm so he will not go into shock, and the medic stays with him until at precisely 1835 at hours, at which time the ambulance arrives and evacuates the mangled Lieutenant.

It has gotten dark and I do not know the time when from my position in the doorway I hear a vehicle's engine being revved from the direction our troops are billeted, so I step out into the street looking for signs of what is happening. I make out the blacked out tail end of a truck loaded with soldiers, moving away from me. I abandon my post and run down the street waving my rifle over my head getting the attention of the troops, who have the driver to stop. Catching up to the truck, I find my whole outfit loaded up and I ask my squad leader, "Why the hell are you leaving me?"

"This truck showed up and we are moving to another area. We forgot all about you being on guard at the edge of town," he replies.

Lt. Evans shouts from the cab, "Forget it and climb on," so the troops assist me in getting aboard and we move out.

CHAPTER
15

RECONNAISSANCE

During basic training we were taught the army has trained teams of scouts, who go on patrols into enemy territory for the purpose of search and destroy, search and capture, along with the task of just gathering information about the enemy. The objective and purpose of reconnaissance at this time in the war is to gather information about the enemy.

The evening I am to go on my first mission, the company commander orders, "Mister Lee, get a couple of volunteers to go with you and scout the area up ahead. Get all the information you can, avoid being detected and only fire your weapons if necessary and be back by 0500 hours."

I tell Lt. Evans, "I don't want to take anyone with me because I think the demise of our previous scouts is because there were too many people. They could not move about undetected; the less movement and noise the better."

I'm told, "You remember, we talked about the practice of using the buddy system in order to protect one another, but if you are serious, go by yourself."

I want to travel as light and inconspicuously as possible, so prior to departing on patrol I give everything I own to one or another buddy for safe keeping. I strip down to my boots, my fatigues and my helmet liner cap. I decide I would rather weather the cold than be encumbered in my movements. I also carry a white handkerchief to be used if necessary to get back through our lines and my hunting knife that I am never without. Of course there is one more item I am never without- my dog tags.

Amidst all the blood and gore we are encountering at this time, I believe it is humorous, when, one evening prior to setting out on my night reconnaissance, Lt. Evans instructs me, "If you come across a gun emplacement go around and around it to see just what it is and how many troops are manning it." I reply, "Yes sir." He and I both knowing full well that if I encounter such a situation, I will make a quick evaluation and get my carcass out of there.

When I receive word I am to go on a reconnaissance, I know I will be up all night and then have to function at my best, on point, all the next day. Then there is the chance, I will go out again the next night, so I sit and attempt to get some sleep, to no avail, because all my buddies file by, shake my hand and tell me in various words.

"I want to say goodbye now, because you and I both know, that one night you are not going to return and then it will be too late to tell you how I feel."

Some ask, "How can you go into enemy territory all alone at night, move around and still be able to find your way back to the unit?"

My reply, "Natural instincts."

When returning from any of these scouting trips I am like a "homing pigeon," thanks to Dad. *Dad knows nothing about longitudes, about latitudes, and about compasses, but he does possess a tremendous amount of common sense, so he teaches me a sort of sixth sense. He takes me into the forest for quite a distance, ties his red handkerchief over my eyes, spins me around a couple of times, then leads me in an unknown direction. I keep track of ascending and descending hills, as well as all stream crossings and when he has me thoroughly lost he takes off the blindfold and says, "All right Lee lead us home."*

I am just a child, but unlike the other boys of my neighborhood, the darkness never bothers me. We have no air conditioning of any type, so on hot stifling nights when it is almost too hot to breath, the kids sleep outside on the grass. The graveyard has acres of beautiful green grass, so I carry my blanket into the cemetery, look around for a nice green patch of grass, and when I locate one, I spread my blanket on the grass and sleep the night.

When I ask my brothers or the neighbor kids, "Why don't you come with me to the cemetery and we can sleep in the nice thick grass," the answer I get is, "Are you nuts? There are all kinds of ghosts and goblins prowling around the graves." I have yet to encounter either:

Being asked, "How can you go into enemy territory at night all by yourself, without a weapon?" My answer, "If I find myself surrounded by Krauts, it is insane to think

I can shoot my way out, I would rather be captured than be dead, because dead sounds so permanent."

I owe my ability to overcome almost every aspect of the situations I encounter in combat to my poor illiterate father. *He shelters all my brothers from as much of the harshness of life, as possible but exposes me to every vile, nasty, thing known. He trains me to kill with a knife, with a gun, with the cutting edge as well as the blunt side of an ax, with a sledge hammer, as well as with my bare hands. He does not realize he is training a frail sickly child to be a soldier, nor does he have any idea he is training me for war?*

Now in my eighteenth year, on the battle front somewhere in Europe and having so much time for thinking, I realize Dad had done me a great favor by forcing me to do those distasteful things during my growing years.

CHAPTER
16

FIELD OF HORROR

The moon illuminates the night with just enough light to allow me to traverse the off road terrain, a few yards off to the side of the slightly elevated asphalt highway as I penetrate deeper and deeper into enemy territory. Approaching the edge of a field, I stop and make my observation of the field before stepping out into it, and I see before me a very weird scene, as if I am having a horrible dream.

I rub my eyes to make sure I am not hallucinating, for I see the field is saturated with small mounds with something sticking up into the air from many of the mounds, and some of these protrusions are making circular movements while others just seem to be moving back and forth. All appears clear with no enemy visible, so I enter the field and discover all the small mounds are human beings of no more than skeletal remains and the stronger of the living among the dead, have their arms extended into the air and are slowly and feebly waving their hands around as if, begging for help or reaching for God, creating a very eerie scene in the moonlight.

Approaching this mass, one individual catches my attention because he is the closest to me. He is lying partially on his back and on his left side, with his mouth open and his dentures are sticking partially out of his mouth. Kneeling beside him I am pushing the teeth back into place when he reaches out feebly with his right hand and grasps my left wrist, with the extraordinary strength possessed by the dying.

Getting his teeth back into his mouth, there is nothing more I can do because I have to continue my mission, so I pry his hand loose and continue on my way. I move through this mass, make a large circle of the area and finding nothing but silence, I return to my unit. The next morning, out in front on point, I walk through this field for the second time. This time I find only death which, on close inspection, the fore mentioned man has joined their ranks.

All the corpses are practically skeletons so they must have died from starvation. I have this feeling of guilt for not being able to assist this throng, during the night but I had neither the means nor the time, for I had my mission to accomplish. The information I gather while on patrol may make a great difference in the number of casualties to my unit in their advance.

Assumption on my part; apparently these people had been on a forced march and had been given a rest break in the field. When the march is resumed, the ones who are too weak to get up are just left to lay there and die. I have the curiosity to wonder and know how many marchers survived and where they have gone. This field scene is one more example of, "Man's inhumanity to man." The image of this scene will be imbedded in my mind forever.

CHAPTER
17

WHAT A TERRIBLE WAY TO DIE

On the return route from a night patrol the deathly still silence of the pre-dawn finds me descending a slope through a forest, about to emerge from the tree line, and as is my habit I scan the clearing before stepping out into it. In the darkness I make out a clump on the ground just a couple of steps from me. Squinting to get better focus in the dim light, I make out a German soldier lying on the ground, in the prone position to the right rear of a machine gun. He has his helmet laying beside him, and his thoughts and concentration must be consuming him as he looks intensely, towards the direction of our lines.

My path is blocked. I can not skirt around him and take a chance of getting shot in the back, so I make a quick observation to see if he is alone. Surely there must be another soldier around somewhere; probably in a vehicle somewhere in the woods to be used for a get away. Seeing nothing in the darkness, with my right hand I slowly reach across my torso, undo the top button of my fatigue shirt, reach into the neckline of my shirt and unsnap the flap of my hunting knife sheathe, praying the snap will not make a click as I unsnap it.

Pulling the knife, I grip it in my right hand, with the blade sticking up from my thumb and forefinger. With a jump, my legs straddle the small of the Kraut's back, and I simultaneously place my left palm under his forehead and pulling his head up I plunge the knife into his throat and jiggle it around until the blood spurts out. He makes a gurgling sound and struggles desperately, but the action is so fast, he has no chance. Letting go of the knife I leave it sticking in his throat and wrap both arms around his head and hang on with all my might, as he wriggles and quivers in his death throes.

When all struggling ceases, I roll him over and retrieve my knife. I have spent the night in total darkness so my eyes are adjusted to the dim night light. As I wipe the blood off the knife, my hands and my sleeves the best I can on his uniform, I take in the details of this grizzly scene and make out the image of a blood covered face of what I believe is a poor young boy, who has no business being in the army. I have just murdered a child who should still be under his mother's care.

Having a hog nice and fat and ready for butchering, I tie a rope around its neck, lead it from the pen to a small mound of corn I have placed under the large tripod, located just above our house and next to the large iron kettle hanging from a small pole tripod. While the pig eats, I remove my shirt, then the blow I give to it's forehead with the blunt edge of my single blade ax does not kill it but does knock it to it's knees. Straddling it's back, I reach under it's snout with my left hand, raise it's head up as far as I can, plunge a large butcher knife into it's throat and jiggle it around until I hit the jugular vein. When I hit it, blood spurts out and I retract the knife and let the pig bleed to death. Going to the kettle filled with boiling water, I wash the blood off my hands and arms. We do not save the blood to make blood pudding or for drinking as is the custom of most families.

The two slaughter houses in town have a room set up for the men to sit around and drink all the fresh warm blood they want, from their own personal cups. This sounds ghoulish, but it is a general practice all around the world. The cups are kept washed and hanging from pegs on the wall. As crude as my dad is, he does not relish this idea and will only do it as a dare. I can not get up the nerve to try drinking the blood even though Dad does his best in his attempts to persuade me, and he tells me, "You need it because of your anemia."

I continue back to the village where I originated my reconnaissance, expecting to report my findings to my company commander, but on arrival I find not a living soul. I am left behind yet another time. Since my canteen is with a buddy, I have no way of ridding myself of all the dried blood that is on my hands and on my fatigue shirt. I also have no weapon, no food or no warm clothing, as I start my trek down the highway, in the direction I hope my unit has taken.

First I spot a cigarette butt, then I spot a wrapper from a chocolate block, and finally I see a C ration can that is still damp inside. This gives me to believe I am on the right track and that my unit has traveled along this highway. Eventually I spot a good sized puddle of water in a ditch and with the blood being dry I pretty well waste my time trying to wash it off with plain cold water.

I walk the rest of the day into the night, when I take shelter in an abandoned house with plans to sleep the night there, but it is so cold I come back outside and walk, mile after chilly mile to keep from freezing. I have no idea how far I have walked, when about mid morning I hear a vehicle approaching, to my rear. I am caught cold turkey right on the paved highway with no place to conceal myself so if the sound is of a German military vehicle I am in big trouble. This is my lucky day, for when I turn around I see an army, deuce and a half ton truck approaching and I flag it down by waving my arms (a total unnecessary motion for I realize the driver would have stopped on his own).

The truck slows down and comes to a stop right next to me, and the three soldiers that emerge from the cab can not believe their eyes, at the sight of such a muddied, bloodied, pathetic looking American soldier standing before them, in the middle of nowhere.

The first words spoken are; "Where are you wounded and how bad is it?"

"It's not my blood, I cut a Kraut's throat," I reply.

"What are you doing out here by yourself?"

"I've been left behind:"

One asks, "Where's your outfit?"

"I don't know."

"Where you going?"

"I'm trying to find my unit."

"And what unit might that be?"

I say, "B company, 101st."

"What a coincidence. We're "B" company cooks, on our way about ten miles down the highway to the next town, to prepare a hot lunch for them, but now it will

119

have to be a hot supper. There's no room in the cab, so climb on back."

"You got any water?" I ask. A canteen is fished out of the cab and I take a long draw from it then hand it back.

After I climb onto the back of the truck with the field stoves and boxes of rations, an open box of cans catches my eye. Removing one, I see I am holding a can of peach wedges and being very hungry. I cut the top out with my general issue can opener that is always, and I stress, always in my pocket. I drink the juice and shake the fruit wedges into my mouth, until the can is empty. Sticking the can top into the empty can I toss the empty can to the side of the road. The flying can catches the eye of one of the cooks. The brakes are slammed on and the truck comes to an abrupt halt. A sergeant comes back to the rear and proceeds to give me a good ass chewing. "What the hell are you doing stealing food? Now some people are going to miss out. I ought to throw your ass out right here. Don't touch anymore."

While this tirade is going on bullhorns are roaring in my head, "When have you eaten last? Yesterday, no, it must have been in the afternoon of the day prior to that, and it's so terrible that a few people are going to miss out on a few peach wedges." What comes out of my mouth? Nothing. I sit there fuming in my silence and cower like a whipped dog?

Arriving at the designated town the first person from my unit to see me yells,"Mister Lee's here and he's wounded. Somone get the medic!" Again I say, "It's not my blood." I am given the same old rhetoric. "A truck arrived not long after you went out to transport us to this new location and we knew you would show." First, I explain the event to Lt. Evans and then I tell my story repeatedly until I am tired of hearing it. Retrieving my gear from the buddy in who's care I had placed it, I find he has taken good care of it. Wearing the bloodied fatigue shirt doesn't appeal to me, but there is not a thing I can do about it for a couple of weeks, until we have enough of a lull to permit the supply truck to show with my duffle bag containing a change of uniforms.

PARDON ME for interrupting, but I have unanswerable questions in my mind. "At what point in my life did I leave my childhood behind? When did my inferiority complex slink away? When did I become a man? Some college athletic teams consist of young adults twenty three years of age, and even older, and their coaches refer to them as, "My kids." No one dare call me a boy or a kid, for although I am just seven month into my eighteenth year no one can dispute I am a man. Yes, I claim I am a man without the years of age to go with it. My apologies for the interruption.

CHAPTER
18

BRITISH AIRMEN

Making my way through a forest of large pine trees at sometime around 0300 hours, I am surprised to come upon a village that I have no idea exists. With the aid of the clear moonlight, I make out the first building on my left to be very long and narrow. There is no movement anywhere. There is only silence, so I move in for a closer scrutiny. Easing open the door of the building to my left I see a long barracks type room and with things being so quiet, I follow up on my curiosity. Pushing the door open enough to go through, I enter and see rows of uniforms hanging along the walls under the oblong small windows. Cots run in two rows crosswise the length of the building and each is occupied by a sleeping person. I think, "Oh my god, I am in a barracks full of sleeping, Germen soldiers," but looking closely at the uniforms, I make out they are uniforms of the, "British Royal Airforce." Gently nudging awake the occupant of the first cot on the right, I inform him, "I'm an American soldier."

"Hey mates, wake up. We're free! The Yankees are here," he yells.

I say, "No you are not free yet. I am just a lone soldier, the main force will be here first thing in the morning to free you. Tell me, why was I able to walk right into town, without encountering any German soldiers?"

He tells me, "The guards got word the Yankees were getting close, so they pulled out yesterday afternoon."

I say in loud voice, "Hang on until morning and you will be free."

I return to my unit and report to Lt. Evans, "I came across a building full of British prisoners. The Krauts have left the town and all is clear so we should encounter no resistance."

Entering the barracks in the morning, I notice, almost every individual is missing a part of his body, from one hand to as many as triple amputees. I say, "You guys must have had rough crashes, to be so beat up."

The individual I talked to during the night tells me, "It is just the opposite of that, we were lucky enough to bail out of our crippled planes and parachute to safety with just a few injuries, but every time one of us broke the rules or provoked a guard, the punishment was having an amputation performed." We are still in the village later in the morning, when war correspondents and photographers from the Stars and Stripes show up. They are referred to me for an accounting of what had transpired during the night and they say, "Tell us how you had to shoot your way into town." Telling them, "The Germans got word we Yankees were getting close so they withdrew from the village, leaving the prisoners unguarded, so I just walked in without encountering anyone." They make the remark, "No, no! Without shooting, there is no story," and they leave.

CHAPTER
19

HIDE FROM GERMAN TROOPS

Moving through the German front battle line into enemy territory, a little before midnight in the pitch darkness, I encounter no enemy troops, so I ignore the noises and activity I hear all around me, cross a paved highway running from my right and angling away from me on my left. After I am into enemy territory sufficiently, encountering nothing, I make a large circle to my left, and start the return trip back to my unit. I am traveling a dry depression, that is probably a run off path for water during wet weather, and approaching the fore mentioned highway elevated by about a four foot embankment, I am facing the opening of a good sized pipe.

Ascending the bank, I cross the road, descend into the depression, and travel a short distance, hearing shouting and voices speaking excitedly in German. I move closer to the sounds, with hopes of finding an opening in the line that I can go through, as I did when I infiltrated their line coming into their territory. In the blackness I make out a saturation of enemy troops practically shoulder to shoulder, with a lot of hustling and bustling going on and I find no visible gaps between the troops. Venturing some distance to the left, in a crouch so as to not be outlined above the pavement, and finding no break in their line, I retrace my steps and do the same on the other side of the depression encountering the same situation.

The sky is lightening for the breaking of dawn, so I know I do not have time to skirt the troops before daybreak. My mission is caput, a complete failure and I am in a ticklish situation. In fact, I am in a real pickle. I retrace my steps back to the depression, follow it back to the pipe and scoot on my stomach feet first into the drain pipe. Had I worn my gear and carried a weapon I would be in big trouble because the pipe is just large enough in diameter for me to squeeze into.

It is late March and I have no way of knowing the temperature, I only know it is cold, and because I travel light the only winter garments I am wearing are my cold weather underwear and my helmet liner scull cap. Lying in the pipe, on my stomach with my legs straight and my arms extended above my head, I have no room to roll from side to side, and I dare not move a muscle for fear of being detected. All the while I am praying to my god that no dogs are present in the area to give away my being there.

I have barely beaten the breaking of dawn and for an unknown period of time, I hear all sorts of activity directly in front of my pipe and above me, as the troops are most likely making an orderly retreat. Only the Lord knows how many vehicles and enemy troops pass not more than three feet above me, causing the pipe to vibrate. I manage to remove my watch from my left wrist but I am so far into the pipe there in not enough light to read the time. While laying there I think, "Whose fault is it that you are in such a predicament? Not poorly educated Mom and Dad, who struggled from the day they were married to raise a family while living in perpetual poverty. You idiot. You have no one to blame but yourself! Think, and think, and think. Turn back the years, do anything to keep the mind alert."

There is a culvert and a very small stream on the other side of Ash road from our house. This culvert houses the opening of a pipe to carry the water of the stream that had been diverted from its natural course through the gully in which we live. This diverting pipe runs downhill in a very straight line, along the side of Ash road, passes under the imaginary Nash street, to another open culvert. The next section of pipe continues from the downhill side of this culvert until it comes to the last culvert at the junction of Ash Road and Fairfield Avenue, then it continues under Fairfield, where the water spills about three feet into St. Clair Run.

The pipe in the culvert across from our house is like a magnet to me, so I enter it, crawl on my hands and knees as far as light permits, then I turn around and make my way out. One day something urges me to crawl the entire length of the pipe from this culvert to the culvert at Nash Street. Knowing Mom will not permit me to do it, I sneak off with my Miner's cap and carbide lamp.

When I am down in the culvert where I cannot be seen by anyone I spit into the carbide, take a match from its water proof container, strike it to flame on the cement culvert wall and light the lamp. I enter the pipe and start my crawl. As I crawl farther and farther into the pipe I realize my childhood ego is too big for me and I become scared, so I turn around and make my way back out. I never give a thought, as to what will happen if I am to get stuck in this pipe. No one is aware of what I am doing or where I am doing it, so imagine the manhunt that would be launched if I do not make it out safely. My skeleton will be trapped or entombed there, unless flushed out with a surge of water. Since my Miner's cap and lamp would be discovered missing, everyone would assume I had gone to one of the many abandoned mines. They would all be searched, but who would think to look in a drain pipe. Although I am not too bright, I have enough sense to never tell anyone what a stupid thing I have attempted.

We live in a hilly, wet area so there are drainage pipes just about everywhere you look, and they have a fascination or attraction that just seems to draw me to them and say, "Crawl me." These drain pipes exist in all sizes from twelve inches in diameter to as large as six feet. I can not pass a sewer or opening without crawling in and seeing how far I can go. At times I crawl, creep or walk several blocks depending on the pipes size and the amount of light from drain grate openings. Sometimes I emerge from the open ends of pipes that culminate in cement culverts, but other times I have to back track. If I do not come to an opening, and the pipe is too small for me to turn around, I back crawl, which is very agonizing, but I become quite good at it.

My favorite pipe is a twenty four inch one at the base of a twenty foot high vertical retainer wall on the south side of Fairfield Avenue. This wall extends from the very edge of the bridge I go down to the water's edge, on the way to school and extends along Fairfield Avenue, for about a hundred

yards. It then terminates at the point where the creek angles
away from the street. To get to this pipe I go over the edge of
the bridge, drop down to a six inch pipe that spans the creek,
at about mid way down the wall, then I drop down to the
narrow walkway. I walk along the walkway at the base of
the wall that extends the length of the wall until I come to
this pipe opening, just before the end of the wall. The pipe
protrudes out a couple of inches from the wall, about two
feet up from the base, so entering the pipe is very easy. Upon
traversing it, I end up in a plain dirt hole in the center of an
empty lot on the north side of the avenue.

I can not get out of the hole because it has a structure over
it to keep out who-knows-what. This structure is square, about
three feet high made of boards, with a flat top. All the boards
have about a half inch crack between them. The men of the
neighborhood place something on the top and use it as a card
table. My brother,Richard is not into crawling sewers, but
does sometimes go with me through this one to retrieve coins
that have fallen through the cracks from the poker games. The
box, in the middle of the empty lot, is at a curve in Fairfield
Avenue, so I often kneel in this structure for hours, looking
through the cracks watching all the wagons, and pedestrians,
coming and going along the thoroughfare. I am spying on the
world, with no one the wiser they are being watched.

Time drags by and I am so cold and stiff I think I will
surely die. "Come on, you are a survivor! Do something."
I move my fingers and wiggle my toes the best I can. I
bend my wrists, my elbows, my ankles and my knees as
far as the pipe permits. I manage to raise and lower my
hips ever so slightly. I turn my head from right to left and
up and down. Because I am lying on my stomach, my
knife sheath has slide around enough that it is digging

into my rib cage and hurting like hell, but with my arms being extended straight out there is nothing I can do to relieve the pain. The rumbling and the muffled sounds persist so I get back to my thinking all the things afore mentioned plus a multitude of other incidents pass through my mind.

I am suffocating; I can not get my breath and desperately need to clear my breathing passages by filling my lungs with tobacco smoke. Leaving the room, I walk about forty feet to a large rock located at the waters edge of the very shallow stream flowing past the building. Tapping a cigarette from the pack, I bring a match to flame by striking it across the outside right leg of my trousers and apply the flame to the Cool Menthol cigarette.

After a couple of puffs on the cigarette I do not get the gratification people addicted to nicotine experience. Instead, I become deathly sick and utilizing the rock for support, I puke my guts out. Being weak and shaky I sit on the rock until my strength returns, then I turn over a few rocks looking for crawdads but have no luck. The opening of the bridge to my right under St. Clair Road beckons me to come and see if everything is in order. Stepping from stone to stone, with occasional slips, I arrive under the bridge and find everything under it is in order just as they were on my last check, so I return to the room and sit down in my desk on the first grade side of the one room schoolhouse.

My desk is to the left of the doorway and is the first desk in the last row, located as close to the door as possible to permit my coming and going without distracting the other students. The teacher is at the front of the room explaining something, (whatever it is teachers explain to students), I could care less.

I am bored so I again leave the room. This trip is to stoke the fire in the wood burning stove in the basement and to dry my pants from my extended smoke break. I have no interest what-so-ever in learning anything. Dad is my ideal and is teaching me realistic things. Why do I have to waste my time in school?

Still suffering with anemia and smoking tobacco keeps my body weight at a minimum. My skin is so taut with the lack of flesh between it and my bones I cannot pucker enough skin to be pinched. I am so small, so puny, so skinny, and so shy that at the end of the school year my teacher has a conference with me and my parents to discuss my situation. I am a dunce but I understand the teacher's statement. Quote: "Lee is so disinterested in learning, I suggest he remain in first grade for another year." I am not yet six years old and I have already been humiliated, because all the other first graders move across the room to the second grade and the second graders all departed for the third grade in another school.

My second year in first grade starts out a clone to the first year. After a couple of months the teacher decides that instead of staying in first and learning nothing, I might as well learn nothing in second grade, so she passes me to the right side of the room where I still learn nothing. I am still a dunce when it comes to learning but am above average with common sense. Dad knows that, like him, I will never be an intellectual so he is teaching me material things, and exposing me to all the vile nasty things I will encounter in life. I can shoot a gun, use a knife, I know how to kill animals and dress the carcasses, I can survive in the wild, etc. What else do I need to know, so my two years in that little school house are wasted years. The teacher decides that two years of me ignoring her is enough, so I am passed on to the third grade in Edgewood Elementary School.

Now that I am thinking about it, "Just what did I learn in all my years of ignoring the teachers?" Not very much. In fifth grade I raise my hand and the teacher asks, "Yes, Lee, what is it?"

"Can I go to the bathroom?" I ask.

She says to the whole class, "Now everyone listen to this. There is a difference in the way you ask. You may go if I give you permission, but only you know if you can go. The saying is. You may if you can and you can if you may."

The teacher is perturbed with the whole class and is standing close to the blackboard admonishing everyone. I turn to the boy sitting to my right and whisper, "Boy is she mad," and she hears me. She stops ranting, goes to her desk, picks up her twelve inch ruler and comes to and stands next to my aisle desk. "Stick out your hands," she orders me. I do so and she takes the ruler and, wop, wop, wop, to the back of each hand. "Now turn them over she says." I do so and get the same treatment to my palms. She says to the whole class, "Remember this, animals go mad and people get angry." Now that she has vented her anger she returns to the front of the room and instead of picking up where she left off, she proceeds to teach.

Lying there cramped in the pipe for what seems an eternity until things are quiet, I finally decide to risk emerging from the pipe. Miraculously I am still alive but attempting to get out of this situation after laying still in freezing weather for so long the muscles of my arms and legs fail to respond. Exerting a lot of effort, slowly and slightly my fingers, my wrists and my toes start to move and eventually I move as many of my joints as I can until they are a little bit operative.

The pipe has a slight rise to it in the direction I am laying with my feet slightly lower than my head, so with all my effort I am unable to move my body forward. Working my elbows and my ankles, in conjunction with my booted feet, I manage ever so slightly, to inch my way backwards until I emerge slowly, feet first from the pipe. With my joints and muscles being so stiff it takes great effort for me to stand. While leaning against the embankment I spend some time working out the stiffness in my body. While working out the stiffness I look at my watch and I see it is 1130 hours. Cautiously straightening up, I look back over the highway for any signs of the enemy, and finding the area is void of any troops, or equipment I again cross the highway and in a crouch I make my way along the depression, expecting a pain in my back at any moment. Judging I am back on our side of the line, I make a direct left and sure enough I arrive at the tiny hamlet where I started my patrol.

The village is void of any living things, I have been left behind once again. This time I have a premonition not to go off left or right looking for my platoon. Instead I retrace our route of the previous day to a larger town we had passed through. Arriving at the town at dusk I find my company has been made whole and the troops are resting while awaiting orders for the next deployment.

This time I do not ask, "Why was I left behind?"

I tell Lt. Evans, "We are lucky for the way things turned out, because had you advanced early this morning there would have been a blood bath. There were hundreds of Germen troops and equipment spread out.

That's why I couldn't get back through their line. It was getting daylight so I had to conceal myself in a pipe until they pulled back, lock stock and barrel. The area is now absolutely void of troops."

Retrieving my gear that has been taken good care of, I find I am ravished so the C rations of ham and lima beans taste delicious. I go into another room and stretch out on the floor. I am so exhausted that I sleep through the entire night. My fingers, my toes, my nose, and my ears tingle for a few days from my exposure to the cold for such a long period of time, but thank the Lord I do not have frost bite and in a few days all is normal.

PARDON ME ONCE AGAIN, but I want to make several points here and I want them to be perfectly clear. I am a mere private first class in combat on the front lines, and I do not run the War. I do not have a daily newspaper delivered and waiting for me in the field or abandoned building when I return from my night patrol, I do not have a radio of which to listen to the news, and no staff officer from headquarters comes to the front line and gives me daily briefings. My war is within my field of vision; that is it, period!

The only encounters I have had with any enemy tanks is the one from which I saved my own life and the one abandoned in the vacant lot. I do not know why, but I think, "What will I do if I encounter a German tank. Anti tank grenades are so heavy and cumbersome I do not know of any being carried by any individual in the whole of my company?" I apologize for my rambling so let's get on with it.

CHAPTER
20

FIREWORKS

About 0100 hours as I stand just inside the tree line on the down slope of a hill looking through the darkness contemplating the best way to accomplish my mission; "get into the city and check for the density of enemy troops," so Leutenant Evans will know what his troops will be encountering in the morning when we take the city. Looking to the bottom of the hill I have a panoramic view of a very large railroad switch yard, then the dark outlines of the buildings in the blacked out city.

Just as I am about to exit the trees, I detect movement around a railroad boxcar sitting alone on the furthest track next to the city. It sits slightly to my right so I can make out three of its corners. Through the darkness it appears people are throwing something up against the sides of the car. Small flames come aglow simultaneously at each corner and the center of the car then small flames flicker as they are placed against the lower portion of the car where slightly larger flames appear and grow in intensity. These flames rapidly grow moving up the sides of the boxcar putting off more light to where I can make out the Germen soldiers as they hastily leave the area.

Evidently the activity I have just witnessed was German soldiers dousing the boxcar with inflammable material because in a very short time the flames completely engulf the car. I watch as the car becomes one large inferno and after it burns for a while I hear sporadic pops. The pops get more frequent and louder, and then the car blows and as I stand there I enjoy the most spectacular fire works show I have ever seen, as red hot shells fly into the air. I watch this scene for a while then call show time over and make the long trek back to my platoon. When challenged with, "Who's there?" I shout, "Mister Lee, I'm coming in." Making my report to Lt. Evans, I tell him, "I did not get into the city but I watched the Krauts burn and destroy a boxcar loaded with ammunition, so it would not fall into our hands."

He tells me, "We could see the sky all aglow and wondered what was burning."

I also inform him, "I figure the soldiers are pulling out and they will all be gone come morning so we should meet no resistance."

"Try to get a little rest because we will be moving out in about an hour," he tells me.

Just after first light all the men of my platoon, including me are spread out among the trees inside the tree line.

Hearing; "Mister Lee." I move closer to Lieutenant Evans.

"Let's see how good your evaluation was. Get into the city and scout around. If you encounter nothing, come back to the rail yard. We will be keeping a close watch for you. If we hear gun shots we will move in as fast as possible. If you don't make an appearance at a half hour after you enter we will assume there is one less Yankee the Germans have to contend with."

After making my way across the tracks of the rail yard I enter the city between two warehouses to the left of the smoldering remains of the boxcar and walk six city blocks towards the heart of the city. Making a right, I proceed another six blocks, make another right, travel back five blocks to the first street I had crossed, make another right and walk with residential buildings on my right and warehouses on my left. I come to the place where I had entered the city. After going between the same warehouses where I entered the city, I step out in the open and wave my rifle over my head, and seeing my signal the troops emerge from the trees, come down the slope, cross the rows of railroad track and join me. We swept through the city encountering nary a soldier or, for that matter, not a living soul so my evaluation was correct.

CHAPTER
21

ON POINT

The purpose of being on point, about three or four hundred yards out in front of the main force when advancing, is to draw enemy fire, thus alerting the troops and preventing an ambush on the main body of troops that follow. If you are lucky and the enemy has a lax moment you may detect them in time to warn your own troops. Going on patrol and being on point are about the two most dangerous and important jobs in an infantry company, so these positions cannot be filled by the meek at heart. These positions are mostly filled by volunteers, proving one has to be an idiot plus one has to be out of one's mind to ask to be put in such precarious situations. When any of my buddies state, "I do not understand when you are on point advancing across a field, how you can walk right up to a hedge row not knowing what is waiting behind it?" My answer, "What other choice do I have?"

On point, I am attired in full battle gear, with two bandoleers of ammunition crisscrossed over my torso as a reserve in case I deplete all the cartridges in my ammunition belt (which I have never done), with a hand grenade hanging from the straps of each bandoleer. If I draw enemy fire, I hit the ground and fire back. My helmet is the most important item I can wear. It is my security blanket.

You say to yourself, "this guy is fabricating stories because when it comes to his helmet, he is in complete contradiction." If you have experienced it, you can attest to the noise a helmet makes when it hits the ground. On patrol I make it a point not to blow my cover and get shot at. Out on point the situation is completely reversed and many a soldier will attest to the fact that had a bullet not defected off his helmet it would have gone right through his skull.

CHAPTER
22

NAKED

If you have ever had a dream where you felt you were walking naked in public, let me explain to you what naked really is. Around mid morning I am out on point, traveling along a ridge, through a sparsely populated forest of enormous pine trees with a gully on my left. Everything is calm and peaceful so I get a little lax. I do not have my helmet strap securely in place.

The calm is shattered when a machine gun opens up on me from about two hundred yards on the opposite ridge of the gully. The good lord is looking out for me because the gunner's timing is off, for just as he pulls the trigger, I step behind a tree causing the bullets to hit the tree trunk instead of me. When I hit the ground at the base of the tree the impact of my head hitting the ground causes my helmet to fall off my head and roll down into the gully.

I scoot my body around in line with the tree trunk, and thank God neither leg has been riddled. Sticking my rifle around the tree trunk periodically, with my right hand I fire at nothing, waiting for the main troops to come to my assistance. The only thing I get each time is another burst of fire from the machine gun. Where is the firing or any other kind of action from my platoon? After firing off several shots and getting no return fire from the machine gunner, I assume he has taken off, so I belly crawl my way back through the trees until I feel it is safe, stand, look around for my troops, and find none, I am left behind and all alone once more. This time there can be no mistake about the direction the troops have taken so I continue on my previous course.

In a couple of hours I am spotted by the rear guard and the word, "Mister Lee's here," gets to Lt. Evans and all movement is stopped. Moving up to the front of the troops to where the Lt. is waiting I ask, "Lt, what the hell happened this time?"

"Where's your helmet?" he asks.

"Back there in the gully."

He tells me, "When the shooting started I didn't want to jeopardize the troops, so we skirted around you. If you are dead there is nothing we can do. We kept hearing sporadic fire and figured you were okay. We knew you'd catch up. Did you knock it out?"

"No," I reply, "The gunner finally took off and God damn it, don't do this to me again."

He snaps, "Get out on point."

I'm fuming. I am angry to the point that, as we say in the army, "I'm pissed off."

Back out on point, concentrating on my job, my anger soon subsides, just like a woman after giving birth, "How soon she forgets."

I am eighteen year old and normally I am gung ho. I am full of vim and vigor and I am an idiot loaded with arrogance and self confidence with the feeling that I can whip the world. I have the feeling I am invulnerable." Without my helmet I feel completely, "NAKED," my manhood seems to have drained out of me and I operate at sub par with the feeling every minute I'm out on point, "I'll take a bullet to the head." This inferior feeling lasts for three days and is alleviated with God's intervention.

The night is clear with lots of moonlight, affording me good visibility as I work my way through the pine trees of a sparsely populated forest. Standing at the edge of a small clearing, scanning it from the treeline before stepping out into it, I can not believe what I think I am seeing. Has the childhood habit of my weird uncanny ability of finding dead bodies kicked in, because I detect what I take to be a body lying before me.

Seeing and believing all is clear, I step out of the trees, advance to the mound, and close inspection proves my thought to be true, for it is the body of a dead American soldier who is laying, in the prone position and the cloth on his back are all bloody. Rolling him over I see he has been shot right through the center of his chest, and checking for vital life signs, I find none. He must have been killed just a short period of time in the evening before my arrival, because the body is still limp and the blood is pliable. Inserting my fingers into the opening of the neckline of his field jacket, I lift out the dog tag chain and expose his dog tags, accompanied by what I make out in the darkness to be a "Star of David." Looking around, I see no trace of a weapon.

The thing that is of most concern to me, and my eyes keep going to it, is the beautifully camouflaged helmet he has on his head and no longer needs. I am in very bad need of one, so without any compunction or second thought I do this terrible, terrible unforgiving act, I confiscate it from him. Since I do not wear a helmet during situations like this I slip my left hand and arm through the chin strap and carry the liner and helmet slung as far back on my left shoulder as it will go and then leaving the body laying there I continue on my way.

Things are uneventful as I come to the village that is the focal point of my patrol, and finding everything quite I move through the village and start my return by way of a large circle, affording me time to think. As I walk I wonder, "What was that soldier doing in this area when he got killed, where is his weapon, and what outfit is he from?" I can not make any sense as to the reason why he is there because as far as I know, I am the only one supposed to be in that area. The conclusion I come to is, (and this debunks my theory that I am the only lone scout in the army,) He is my counter part and, the epitome of the subject of this book, "THE UNRECOGNIZED AND FORGOTTEN SCOUT." On my arrival back at my platoon I report my find to Lt. Evans who also can make no sense of the situation. At first light of the morning, I don the helmet with liner and feel my self esteem surge back into me. I silently say, "Thank you, whoever you were." We move out in a slightly different direction than the location of the dead soldier, so I do not know any more about him.

CHAPTER
23

28 GERMAN PRISONERS

The Germans are in complete route so we are riding on our six support tanks, in swift pursuit. Everyone but me stands in back of the turret, where they feel they have protection from enemy fire. Having to be out in front, I sit at my favorite position, astraddle the machine gun guard on the front of the tank. Everybody tells me, "You'r crazy! Up there you have no protection from enemy gun fire. At least back here we have the turret for protection." The only fallacy in that is, not everyone can get a good, secure hand grip on the turret. When one tank tread is locked and the tank makes a sharp turn, the tank pivots so fast some troops lose there grip, and are slung from the tank just like a fishing hook and sinker is cast from a fishing rod. The natural instinct when flying through the air is to grab on to something and the only thing available in this situation is your rifle, so when you grip it and hit the ground or the pavement you get busted knuckles. I see this happen time and time again.

Traveling a paved highway following along atop the knoll of a hill, one of the tankers who is standing in the open hatch of the turret of the lead tank, on which I am riding, thinks he sees activity on the knoll of the hill on the other side of the valley, to our right. The tanks come to a halt and Lt. Evans, who is riding the same tank with me, is informed of the tanker's observation and orders, "Mister Lee, go check it out and take the first squad with you for back up."

With me leading the way we descend the slope to the bottom of the valley, cross a small stream, start up the other hill and come to a wagon road with the upgrade to our right. The squad leader has us follow the road up, and when we come to a cutout in the hill to allow for wagons to pass. I say to him. "I'll go over the bank here and take a look."

"No, We'll follow up the road." He is just showing his authority, because he has a slight resentment of me being a private, having the power to override a staff sergeant. I am assigned to the first squad, so the normal order would be to the squad leader, "Sergeant, take your squad and Mister Lee and go check it out." Notice the order is, "Mister Lee, go check it out and take the first squad with you for back up."

We proceed up the road a couple of hundred yards where he orders me, "Go over the bank and take a look." When the men of the squad have spread out along the bank to give me cover, I go up and over the bank, knowing this is the very same situation that got my predecessor killed. I have stepped into a field, that being on the knoll of the hill, has a slight roll to it with the planting row mounds running from my left to my right. Moving along in a crouch, directly ahead of me I see the upper portion of a tree so I straighten up and see a group of German soldiers clustered under it. Without taking good aim I fire off a shot from my rifle and all hell brakes loose.

They must have been waiting for us, because there is no time laps from my shot to their volume of return fire, with the bullets passing so close to my ears, they create a lot of, "Ping, pings and zing, zings," like the sound made by a swarm of buzzing bees. I hit the ground and lay in the depression between the rows, waving for my back up to move up. Nothing happens so after a while, back crawling I make my way back and down the bank to the dirt road to find there is not a soul to be found. I have been abandoned. As I ponder what to do I look across the valley and see the tanks have proceeded down the highway and are out of sight, so I begin my trek down the wagon road, with the hope of somewhere meeting up with my outfit. As I approach the fore mentioned cut out, I hear the squad leader, procrastinating verbally, to his men, "What are we going to do now that they got Mister Lee?" Had I been a Kraut I could have wiped out the bunch.

Stepping into view, I say, "Here I am," and they exclaim in unison, "No way! We saw you get killed." I do not have a feeling of animosity against any of them for leaving me, because I know they wanted, only not to get killed. I take command of the situation and tell the sergeant, "I'll go up here and take another look, from this angle of the field," and a corporal volunteers to go with me. I, of all people, realize and appreciate the great courage it took for him to volunteer. The two of us go over the bank, and moving in a crouch, we move some distance out into the field. I tell him, "Cover me while I take a look." I straighten up and seeing nothing, we again move forward in a crouch and I again tell him, "Cover me."

Again I see no movement, so I move farther into the field, and in my exuberance, and anticipation of encountering the enemy, I move ahead until I can no longer be seen by my back up man. All of a sudden just a couple of steps ahead of me, up comes four hands and two helmets. Then to the right and left of these, more hands and more helmets appear; seemingly out of nowhere. I have almost stepped in a foxhole containing the enemy. I call out in German, "Come here," and a total of twenty eight Germen soldiers emerge out of the fox holes. I have approached them at about mid point of fifteen holes, with one being empty. I am of German decent so I understand a little German. Having them assembled, I detect no weapons so I order in broken German, "Drop all of your weapons," and I am totally amassed and surprised, to hear the German sergeant reply in better American English than my own, "All our weapons have been left in the foxholes."

Inquiring as to why they have surrendered, the sergeant points and tells me, "Our lieutenant has been killed just a short time earlier, and his body is under that tree in the field." The revelation, I had been so lucky to have killed their officer, when I had fired that random shot, is beyond my belief, and my wildest dream.

The Sgt. continues, "We are without a leader and almost out of ammunition; we talked it over, and decided, if we put up a feeble fight and completely deplete our ammo, we will all be killed. It's time this stupid war is over. What did our lieutenant die for? It will be better to surrender and be a prisoner than be dead." This is an echo of my very same words.

Keeping the prisoners covered with my rifle pointed at them, I have them follow me, as I back up to within sight of my back up man, I call out to him, "Wave the others to come forward and see what we have." This he does; and when they get to us, you could never see a braver bunch of soldiers, as they slap around the prisoners, relieving them of their watches and their jewelry. The captured Sergeant is concerned about the body of their officer lying under the tree and I tell him, "We cannot carry him, so leave him and he will be picked up in a short while." We do not retrieve their weapons from the fox holes for, as I stated before, we are not the least bit interested in collecting souvenirs. I did not think to ask, "What are you soldiers doing in foxholes, out here in the middle of nowhere, guarding nothing?"

The lord is looking after us this day; because as it turns out, my squad leader had made the right decision in taking us to another location for me to go over the bank to make my observation. Had I crossed the field at the cut out and found the empty fox holes, I would have waved the squad forward, setting us up for a possible ambush, because the holes had not been permanently vacated, only empty at the time. We march the prisoners down the wagon road into a small town where we unite with our platoon. My squad leader reports to Lt. Evans, "Mister Lee killed a Kraut Lt. We found no weapons and we took these Krauts prisoners." Not one word is spoken about the details of the skirmish and I keep mum for it is not my nature to humiliate anyone. This time I get no rhetoric's about, "We take no prisoners."

The prisoners are put in an empty building under guard and Lt. Evans reports to the control post, "I have a dead German officer and 28 prisoners to be picked up." The next morning a truck arrives with a driver and several other soldiers. One of the squad members who was along on the skirmish is designated to show the pick up crew just where the body is located. Upon the return of the retrieving detail, the prisoners are loaded onto the truck and it then departs for the rear. With the troops loaded back on the six tanks, we moves out in the direction of our next destination. Not a word is ever spoken about me being abandoned.

CHAPTER
24

SACRIFICIAL LAMB

Since we are not encountering any mass of Kraut resistance, the company is usually split up, with each platoon operating on its own, in order to cover a larger area as we advance. Lt. Evans summons me and passes the word, "Mister Lee, I summoned you here along with all the platoon leaders, to inform them I have been instructed, that the Krauts are on the run, so try keeping casualties to a minimum. One way to accomplish this is, instead of spreading out and moving in to clear a town, lay back and send your point in to see if he draws fire."

Now, I have the same fear as any other soldier, and I also do not have any more or less courage than my fellow troops, but being told I am going to be a sacrificial lamb should create a shock to my nerves. This is the way we have already been operating, so it is just routine information to me.

CHAPTER
25

SHOOT COMPANY COMMANDER

2245 hours finds Lt. Evans explaining to me, "Mister Lee, we have to move into the town up ahead tonight, so move out; just follow the paved highway and it will take you right to the town." It is around 2300 hours when I move out in a pitch black night, so dark I have to travel on the pavement, for there is no way I can see to traverse the off road terrain as I usually do when on point. About 0100 hours, all of a sudden simultaneously, from just a few yards to my front and to both sides I hear the words shouted, "WHO IS THERE," and I stop dead in my tracks. My blood seems to boil and freeze at the same time; it is amazing how fast the human mind can analyze a situation, and I make the following assumptions in a fraction of a second.

The words are not the words used by American soldiers, to challenge someone. The words we had always been taught were, "WHO'S THERE" or "WHO GOES THERE," not, and I reiterate "WHO IS THERE." I think, "Oh, my God; I'm right in the midst of a bunch of

Krauts, but it is so dark they can't see me, so if I don't move they might think it is an animal they hear." The second challenge is issued, and I still do not move as the stories told by my fellow combatants swirls through my mind "of how German patrols behind our lines, answered in perfect English when challenged." I also remember how the Kraut sergeant had answered me in perfect American. Just as the third challenge is issued these things happen simultaneously.

From back in the distance my company commander, Lt. Evans, shouts, "B company." The American troops in whose's midst I am standing, yells, "Advance and be recognized." At this precise moment the clouds part enough to create a hole that allows the bright moonbeams to illuminate me, just as if I were standing in the beam of a center stage spotlight in a theatre. These friendly troops are taken aback with amazement, to see me standing there, right in their midst and they exclaim in unison, "What the hell are you doing standing here among us! We didn't hear you, but we were challenging the noise in the distance."

When my company approaches to where these other troops are standing, and I and all the troops have commingled around us, I face my company commander and I ask, "Lt." Did you know we were to meet up with friendly troops and didn't pass the information on to me?"

"Yes I did and I should have told you."

In my rage and heat of the moment, with a raised voice I say loud and clear, almost in a shout, right in front of all the troops gathered around us, "Lt., if you ever do that to me again I'll shoot your ass." I am just a private first class, so imagine what the consequences can be for me for making such a threatening statement to an officer if the Lieutenant so desires. Being the man I respect more than any other for his courage and leadership, he replies, also in a clear loud voice that everyone can hear, "Don't worry Mister Lee. It will never happen again."

CHAPTER
26

TANK ATTACK IN FOREST

Traveling through a sparsely treed forest, with most of the tree trunks being about a foot in diameter, I am out on point moving along the side of a hill and as it is getting twilight Lieutenant Evans motions me back to him and tells me, "We are done for the night." I can not understand why they are there, but the area has several dugouts in the ground that are about twenty feet square by four feet deep and each is covered with a camouflage net. We all take shelter under the nets, by way of a sloped entrance, finding we can lay or sit, but not stand. We spent the night there, and when all have forced down their breakfast of C- rations I am again out on point, moving through the trees.

As I advance, about three hundred yards out in front of Lt. Evans, the trees become denser and larger. I keep looking down into the valley on my left, and watch our six support tanks moving along parallel to us on the highway and wonder, "Why are we making our way through these trees on the side of a hill when we could be riding on those tanks?" All of a sudden the trees start exploding around me, so I hit the ground fast, up against the base of a tree trunk. Some instinct has me lay there with my body between the tree trunk and the tanks. This position probably saves my life because the projectile's momentum splits the tree trunks, and travels some distance before exploding. When the shelling ceases and the troops come up to me, they see all the shattered trees and can not believe I am not dead, let alone not having one scratch on me. When contact is made, the tanks column commander remarks, "We saw what we thought were Germans moving through the trees, so we opened up, sorry about that." To the tankers, my passing from tree to tree must have created an optical allusion of many people moving, but they had to know, their tanks and our troops were moving parallel with each other.

Back on point, my mind is boggled with silly thoughts such as, "I must be one hell of a warrior, that I can be mistook for a whole group of enemy soldiers."

2. "This can not be topped; one individual drawing the cannon fire of six tanks; how can we possibly win the war when six tanks cannot kill one skinny soldier?"

3. "How could I have possibly imagined, when I was building these very same tanks in the Baldwin Locomotive defense plant as a sixteen and seventeen year old that, some day they would be turned on me?"

4. I also ponder the question, "With friendly troops such as these tankers, who needs enemies?"

CHAPTER
27

SILENCE BUNKER

As our troop loaded tanks approach a small town, all the soldiers dismount and walk along both sides of the tanks, through the town with rifles at the ready, in case we meet any resistance. I am walking on the left, and next to the lead tank. Passing the last building on the left, as is my habit, I make a panoramic view of the valley. The highway has a steep decent to the valley floor and runs as straight as an arrow down the center of the valley, as far as the eye can see. On the right, a field rises at a gentle slope until meeting the tree line of the hill in the distance. To the left a very shallow ditch runs between the highway and an open field that has a gentle slope for about a hundred yards then rises steeply to the very dense tree line.

All looks clear and serene, so we proceed down the slope. Four of the tanks with the dismounted troops have cleared the last building and the other two tanks and soldiers are still in town at the upper end of the slope. The lead tank just reaches the leveling off area of the highway when a burst of machine gun fire erupts from up in the tree line to our left.

For some unexplainable reason I am the only soldier walking to the left of the lead tank. The shells pass very close over my head, hitting the turret of the lead tank right next to me. I hit the shallow ditch fast; lay on my left side and watch burst after burst of fire come from the same spot, with every few rounds being a tracer.

It appears as if the machine gun is just resting on the ground between the trees as it fires, so the tank gunner of the lead tank swivels the turret around and fires one shot that I think has split my head open, for the muzzle of the cannon is directly over me. The tank commander rises up in the opening of the turret and proclaims, "Direct hit!" When the dust created by the shell's explosion clears, the machine gun gives another burst and, looking closely, I make out what looks like the burst of the machine gun is coming from a cement wall; it is a bunker. After each burst, the charade continues, with the same results.

One of the tracer slugs hits the tank, ricochets up in the air and slightly back towards the woods. It loses its momentum, causing it to fall to where I am laying in the ditch. It comes to rest on my left inside thigh, burning me like mad, so I brushed it off real fast with my right hand, never thinking about such a silly thing as waiting for it to cool and picking it up as a souvenir.

Taxing my feeble mind, I analyze the situation thusly. I am exposed to the gunfire so if the gunner in the bunker lowers his aim, I am a goner. Something has to be done. As soon as the tanker fires his next shot I will get out of here. A shot from the lead tank's big gun creates this desired dust at the bunker. Taking advantage of this, I get up and dash across the pavement and around the tank. Making my way along the tanks, I get back to the house that is on the gunner's side of the highway. Entering the house, I find Lt. Evans and some of my platoon are there watching the whole episode through several windows. One of the troops remarks, "My brother is out there, and if he gets killed it will surely kill my mother, because I have already lost two brothers."

With the shooting still going on, Lt. Evans says, "Mr. Lee, I'm glad you got here, we are at a stalemate. We can't stay here all day, and we have to move on to the next town, so do something about that gun." There is nothing between the house and the woods so I go up the hill, into the forest, finding the distance much greater than I had anticipated, and a lot of time is consumed before I am able to work my way to the right, towards the gunner. As I get closer I make out the image through the trees of a very large concrete structure and, looking to my right into the valley, I can see the tankers periodically fire in my direction. I hear the explosions as the shells hit the bunker. I say to myself, "The tankers cannot be aware of my endeavor to silence the gun so if they detect my movement, I hope they do not again make the assumption that I am a German soldier?"

On closure approach, I make out the back end of a vehicle and a German soldier, who yells something in German as he runs towards the vehicle. I make his raised, excited voice in German out to be, "Come here quick, the Yankees are coming." A soldier emerges from the bunker and as he moves towards the vehicle I fire a shot with my rifle that I am carrying at the ready. The soldier falls, so I think I hit him, and the fore-mentioned soldier jumps onto the vehicle. He takes off. with me firing successive shots at the moving vehicle, but do no good because of all the trees. Running to the bunker and finding the door open, I stand next to the door with my back to the wall, reach across with my left hand, and remove a grenade from my right bandoleer. With my right hand, I pull the activating pin and release the lever, count to three, swivel my body around and toss the grenade through the doorway. Boy, oh boy! I almost held the grenade too long because it no more than clears the doorway until it explodes. With the explosion of the grenade a soldier is blown through the doorway, landing on his stomach with his feet still in the doorway. Stepping over his legs I rush in to find the place empty.

The Germen soldiers were leaving in such haste they left the machine gun in place, and as I man it, looking through the slot I see the tanks moving. I see no troops on them, so they must be walking on the far side of the tanks. Moving the machine gun back and forth through it's range I find it has a very limited field of fire, covering only a small portion of the valley and the highway running through it. Turning around to leave the bunker, I walk to the door and scrutinize the soldier laying face down, partially in and partially out of the doorway. The exposed portion of his neck is all bloody, the upper portion of his uniform is saturated with "holes," and the cloth on his back are moving ever so slightly. The grenade must have just cleared his shoulders when it exploded. I am lucky the grenade got past him and didn't hit him in the chest, and bounce back out the door and blow me up.

Rolling him over onto his back, and straightening his legs out from up against the door frame, I see the front of his uniform looks perfectly normal, his lips have blood on them and he is breathing ever so slightly; he is alive. He is no more than a child in a soldiers uniform, his wide open eyes staring at me, and I see they are filled with what I believe is fear, being caused by either the fear of dying or by the fear I will shoot him.

Kneeling next to his right side, I try to sooth his pain and fear by squeezing his right hand with my left hand and stroking his left check with the fingers of my right hand as I tell him in English, "Try to relax, you do not have to be afraid of me, and you will be alright as soon as I can have our medics come and take care of you." He may or he may not understand what I am saying, but as I hold and squeeze his right hand, and continue to brush his cheek he sort of relaxes and after a few minutes his body becomes still; he has met his maker:

Moving to the other Kraut who is also laying face down, I roll him over and see the bullet has entered his torso under and slightly to the rear of his left armpit and exited on the right side of his chest, just to the front of his armpit, and he is dead. I am nauseated to see I have just killed two more youngsters. Are there no men of age left in the German Army? I am sickened as the thought goes through my mind, "I'm becoming quite good at killing children."

Departing this scene I notice the terrain down to the field is very steep and rugged, so I follow the dirt road the enemy vehicle has taken along the ridge and as I travel I think, "Since the machine gun was doing no damage to the tanks why didn't Lt. Evans have the troops move to the far side of them and stay concealed as the tanks move down the valley and out of the guns range?"

Hitler must have known in his warped mind, he is living a pipe dream that would eventually be shattered. Why else would he construct such a huge bunker right in the heartland of Germany, if he didn't visualize liberating forces some day moving down that highway?" It is evident; the bunker had been constructed years earlier, when the trees were small, and had since grown large enough to obscure it from view. I also think, "What a terrible waste of flawed, defensive planning and construction, to house one little gun covering such a restricted area."

My thoughts go back to the dying German soldier in the doorway of the bunker. "What the hell is the matter with you; a hardened killer, that would perform such an act of kindness to that dying enemy soldier who just minutes before was doing his best to kill you?" That scene must be the most <u>stupid</u>, the most <u>dramatic,</u> and the most <u>pathetic</u> scene in the annuls of warfare; you dare not ever describe that act to the other troops, for the battle hardened combatants will exclaim, "Why didn't you just shoot the little bastard," and you will be the laughing stock of the platoon? But, I am not the average hate filled combatant; I am me and have neither the hate nor the heart for killing but I will continue to do what must be done.

It is dusk when I come to a point where the road continues on, with a branch going down the hill to my right. I take the downhill branch, that leads me to the paved highway with the town to my immediate left. Entering the town I find not a trace of civilians, troops, or tanks, so I move through town until a sentry calls out, "Mr. Lee is here."

I ask Lt. Evans, "What happened?"

He tells me, "The tankers finely knocked out the gun, so we moved on. I knew you would show up."

"Well they didn't knock it out," I say, "The gun crew heard me coming and I killed one with my rifle and another with a grenade, and another one got away in a vehicle." Lt. Evans instructs his radio man to report the two dead soldiers to the command post.

CHAPTER
28

LEFT BEHIND

Things are in a lull on this particular day, so we move into an abandoned small town to await further orders on our pursuit of the enemy. A staff officer comes forward to consult with Lt. Evans, and while he is giving his briefing we have use of his jeep and driver. It is getting dusk in the evening when we utilize his jeep to post me on guard at an unknown distance over a paved highway, to a location that is what we call, (out in the boondocks.) Dismounting from the jeep, I go into a one man roadside guard shack and the sergeant instructs me, "Keep a lookout for any unusual activity." I ask, "What am I supposed to do if I see anything?"

"I don't know; you'll be relieved in a couple of hours."

I have no phone so I do not know what I am supposed to do in case the enemy shows up. When darkness sets in things liven up with the onset of artillery fire from both sides. As the hours drag by and no relief shows, the constant flashes and sounds of the artillery pieces, the swishing of projectiles passing overhead, and the loneliness make the night become a clone of hallucinations, to the night in no-man's land.

Remaining in the shack all night, at daybreak with still no relief guards showing up, I abandon the shack and make the long trek back to the town, that is now more abandoned than ever. I find not a trace of any soldiers or living things. Once again I start walking in the direction I figured the troops have gone. I know the direction we entered the town the day before so I exit the town following the highway out the other end. As I walk, I occasionally find a discarded cigarette butt, so my hopes are high that they were thrown away by smokers of my unit. I am lucky that I carried all my equipment with me when I went on guard, so I am able to eat C-rations from my gas mask pouch.

As the darkness of night is about to engulf me, I am weary from the lack of sleep and from walking such a great distance all day, so I seek shelter for the night. There is not a trace of a building anywhere that I can see, so I move off the highway to a tree that bears no leaves but it still gives me a sense of shelter. Removing all my gear, I place my gas mask pouch on the ground and dine on the contents of a box of K rations. Then I don my rain poncho over my field jacket, lay down and curl up on the hard, bare, cold ground. I am able to get some relief from the cold by spreading my overcoat that I have been carrying tucked under the back of my belt, along with my poncho, over me like a blanket. I turn from side to side, I sit with my back up against the tree trunk, and when I can not tolerate the situation any longer I put on my overcoat and all my gear. Then I continue my trek on the highway. I walk mile after weary mile throughout the remainder of the night, through all of the morning until about mid afternoon my luck changes, when I hear a vehicle approaching from my rear. I flag down an army ¾ ton truck traveling in my direction. The only occupant in the truck is the driver who asks, "What the hell are you doing out here in the middle of nowhere?"

"I've been left behind by my unit."

"Get in, I'll take you to the command post."

I am dropped off at the regimental command post of the 101st infantry regiment and a clerk contacts my company by field phone. "B" company is broken up and operating in single platoons, and mine is not a great distance from where I am located, so a jeep gets me joined up with my platoon late in evening.

I ask, "Why was I left behind this time?" My squad leader tells me, "You were not forgotten but a truck showed up with orders to move to this location immediately, so we did not have time to come pick you up. We knew you would show, as you always do." I tell him, "God damn it, this is happening too often and one of these times it will be a disaster for me." I did not press the issue, but I know I was just plain forgotten, because it would not have taken long for the truck to go to the shack and pick me up.

CHAPTER
29

FIND SECOND PLATOON

Early morning finds the first and second platoons of my company, deployed inside the tree line at the edge of a field, between us and the first buildings of a large city. The sun is just about to make its appearance and we can see it is going to be a beautiful day weather-wise. Lt. Evans instructs the second platoon leader, "My platoon will clear the right half of the city and you will take the left half." Then he gives his order, "Mister Lee, get into town and clear a section for us to move in." I hunch over in a crouch, with my rifle across the front of my body at the ready and advance across the field expecting, "Who-knows-what?" Encountering no resistance, I enter the city between a couple of buildings, make a round of one block, and back at the space between the buildings. I signal the troops in.

Out in front, advancing down a street for perhaps ten city blocks clearing buildings, Lt. Evans motions me back and orders, "Go back and locate the second platoon and find out what kind of resistance they are encountering."

Retracing our route back about five blocks I turn to my right, go to the third street and seeing no one, I figure the second platoon has already passed on into town. I make another right and proceed for a number of blocks in the direction I think the troops have taken. When I still have not sighted anyone I decide to cut over one more street.

Attempting to go through a barn to my left, I cannot get the door open. I go along the barn wall to the right, ascend three concrete steps, unlatch a gate and move to the edge of the building. Rounding the corner of the barn, I move to the end of the barn and make my observation of the area. Crossing about fifteen feet of grass yard, to a solid wooden board fence about five feet high, I am about to climb over the fence when I hear this clop, clop, clop, so I freeze in a crouched position. There is one board missing in the fence space, so as I peer through the opening, I see this contingent of about fifty German soldiers, led by an officer, marching down the cobblestone street moving from my right to my left. There is not more than ten feet between me and the soldiers because there is just the fence and no sidewalk between us. Figuring they are making an orderly withdrawal, I realize I am in hostile territory.

I thank my god for creating me a coward, for had I attempted anything heroic I am a dead man. As soon as the contingent of soldiers pass I turn around, still in a crouch, to make tracks back around the barn, when to my amazement, the back door to the barn opens and out steps three German soldiers. It is a bright morning with the sun being a fire ball to my back; shining right into and blinding the three soldiers eyes. A split second elapses before they adjusted to the glare. Seeing I have my rifle pointed, point blank at them, they are so stunned that the only one with a rifle drops it, and they raise their hands above their heads. Here are three grown-up full-fledged men soldiers I had wondered about.

This is another of my unexplainable survivals, for I figure I have just hid from the three Germans in the barn not more than fifteen feet to my rear as I watched the formation march by on the other side of the fence. I take them around the barn to the street just in time to see some American troops about three blocks back the way I had come. I have the prisoners stay out of sight in the cut out to the barn entrance and expose myself to the advancing troops, in plenty of time for them to recognize me as one of their own. They turn out to be the evasive second platoon, led by the lieutenant who had ordered me to return the wine sack. When they approach me, the second Lieutenant asks. "What the hell are you doing in this section of town?" The soldiers of the platoon can not believe there can be a GI in the section of town still to be cleared.

I tell the Lieutenant, "I just watched about fifty Krauts march down the street on the other side of the barn, and I have three prisoners waiting around the corner in the entrance to the barn." Backing up a few steps, I have the three prisoners come out onto the street and I turn them over to the Lieutenant. I state my mission to him and he tells me, "We have not encountered any resistance," so with the information I am seeking, I start my return to my platoon. I have gone about a half of a block on the way back to my platoon, when I hear a volume of three rifle shots, and my mind vibrates with the words, "We take no prisoners." Back with my platoon I explain to

Lt. Evans what had transpired, without mentioning the rifle shots.

Perhaps the reason I do not develop a hatred for the German soldier, is the fact that I entered combat after the brunt of attacks, before and right at the almost conclusion of the "BULGE." I feel only pity for every enemy soldier I kill. I also feel they are only doing their job, the same as me. I say, "Things could have been reversed." I pray I can stand corrected, but my belief is, had our government decided to brain wash our youth into thinking we could take over the world, millions of them would have signed up for my imaginary, "Youth of America Groups."

CHAPTER
30

HODGEPODGE

This story will offend multitudes, but I have to tell it like it is from my personal point of view, experiences, and way of thinking at the time souvenirs were available. I reiterate, these are <u>my own personal thoughts</u>. By this time in the war some troops have already returned home bearing enemy rifles, helmets, etc, and these items are displayed by their proud owners. I say these articles were not acquired by the true fighting, infantry soldier. The true combatant, who engaged and physically fought the enemy, had to be agile so he traveled as light as possible. With all your battle gear, picking up a discarded enemy rifle is utterly unthinkable.

As the fighting infantrymen push the enemy back and follow in close pursuit, the rear echelon fills the void left by these troops, riding in their mess trucks, their supply trucks, and their numerous other headquarter personnel vehicles. Last but not least, the artillery, God bless them; move up with the towing vehicle's, pulling the large weapons to a more forward position. The personnel riding in all these vehicles stop and load up on all types of items, to have for mementoes of the war. To me, picking up a discarded weapon or any other item, is not a souvenir. A souvenir should be an item with a story behind it; otherwise it is just something you found.

All through the ages volumes have been written about soldiers keeping logs and journals, so I want to set the record straight on this topic by stating some facts taken from my mind's warped way of thinking. I reiterate; I believe it is ludicrous to think a truly fighting soldier, has time for such nonsense. First of all you travel as light as possible, so you do not carry pencil and paper. You ask, "How heavy can a little paper and a pencil be?" Well, every little thing adds up and you know it only took that one straw to break the camel's back. You have nowhere to carry sheets of paper and keep them dry so writing material is kept stashed in your duffle bag on the supply truck back at the rear echelon and only available to you when the situation is absolutely safe enough for the supply truck to come forward, up close to the front line.

A month or six weeks may elapse without the pleasure of sleeping in a building. You spend the bitter cold days on the move so you can not write notes. The nights when you get a chance to rest, you dare not have a light because this has been the demise of many a soldier. You say this is a contradiction from back at burning one straw after the other. That situation was right in the middle of a town and did not pose a danger from the enemy.

You are opening and eating cold C rations that occupies the space in your gas mask pouch once filled by your gas mask. The gas mask is now back on the supply truck because, you take the chance you will not encounter any gas. Food is much more essential to you than useless paper and pencil. You are on the move all the time, so you are always hound dog tired and take advantage of every lull period to catch up on all the rest you can, by taking cat naps. You may go as many as five days and nights without any decent sleep. Anyone taking umbrage with my statements, please feel free to voice your opinion, for these are my convictions and I believe I can withstand the tirade.

Being informed of an evening that you will be engaging the enemy the next morning, most soldier's minds are possessed with fear. Picture your mindset after being informed of an evening that you are going into battle the next morning. Knowing you will be engaging the enemy the next morning in itself is enough to shatter one's nerves, as you have all night to think about whether you will be killed the next day. While all this is going on, you shiver constantly from the cold, all the while hugging your torso, clapping your hand and banging your boots with your rifle butt, checking for feeling in your feet. My solution for not letting the stress and fear factor get the better of me, when knowing we will be engaging the enemy the next morning is to blank it all out of my mind, by going to sleep.

I want to make it perfectly clear that this article on press coverage is derived from my own personal experiences, and in no way casts a doubt on the truly brave war correspondents. I back up my veracity, with the episode of British airmen and the following incident.

The time is around 0600 hours and the troops of the whole company are spread out at the edge of trees looking at a large city when Lieutenant Evans orders, "Mister Lee, get into town and clear enough area so we can move in." Moving across the field in a crouch, entering the city between two buildings with no problems, I make a round of several blocks, encounter nothing of mention. Back at my point of entry, I tie my white handkerchief to the muzzle of my rifle and give the signal, "all is clear," so the troops move in. When the troops have all entered and the city is secure, press photographers and correspondents show up and tell lieutenant Evans, "Take your troops back out of town and come back in firing their weapons, so we can take action pictures."

Lt. Evans tells them, "Get lost because my men have had a hard day and are tired and need some rest." All the troops have a great respect for the company commander for this decision but, a lot of fake glory and fake history is lost to posterity.

When a soldier, exceeds the limits of his tolerance for fear, his nerves shatter and transforms him into a whimpering simpering idiot. He breaks down and he shakes with convulsions, and he cries and whimpers like a baby. It is a pitiful sight to witness and the men who reach this state of mind are taken out of combat. Rehabilitated and returned to action, as soon as they hear the first shot, they break down all over again. No man is condemned for this disorder because we all know, "But for the grace of God, there goes I."

One of my buddies from basic training hits the low and is evacuated. About a week later he returns and on hearing the first explosion of a rifle, he regresses, so his fighting days are over.

Though I am scared to death when advancing into battle, I reiterate that I take a couple of gulps and swallow what I think is my heart, then move on and get the job done. Visualize being told; at 1800 hours you will be facing the death squad at daylight. You have all night to think about this, and with each passing hour the fear grows.

A battle hardened corporal in my platoon breaks and runs. He is tackled and put on notice, "If you ever run again we'll shoot you in the back." He has not reached the low of battle fatigue; he is just running scared. Returning to his position he functions properly from then on. This episode is never brought up to him again.

Letters from my girl friend are becoming less and less frequent, with each empty mail call being a disappointment. I do not think too much about the lapses, because I can not say I am a consistent letter writer due to the circumstances I am in. Then one day mail call has a much anticipated letter for me, from my girl friend. I open the envelope and there it is.

My dearest Lee;
I am sorry but I cannot wait, I'm getting married next week.
The best of luck to you
L-----

My world comes to an end, creating a terrible pain in my chest. Fortunately, I do not have much time to dwell on my misfortune, due to going on a patrol that evening and I have time to think, "How lucky I am, not to have gotten married, before entering the army, and being encumbered the rest of my life, with an unloving wife." With this thought in mind, it takes but a few hours for me to get back to normal.

CHAPTER
31

STRAFINGS

The troops of my company are walking single file on each side of a paved highway that is littered with disabled German army vehicles. We look skyward and cheer as several "P-38" planes pass overhead. When they get past us we watch one make a "U" turn and come back towards us. All of a sudden the plane goes into a dive and its machine guns open up on us. We hit the pavement fast. I, and I assume everyone else, retained what we had learned in basic training, "In a strafing hit the ground crosswise of the plane, thus exposing a minimal amount of your body to the bullets." Miraculously during all this shooting no one is hit and when contact is established, we get, "Sorry about that, I saw all those German vehicles and thought you were German soldiers."

Traveling along the ridge of a hill I am out in front of the troop and passing between a series of boulders three to four feet high. Looking ahead I make out what I think is the front view of a German fighter plane coming at me very low, just high enough in the air to clear the ridge. I yell, "Everyone down," and I dive behind a boulder to my right. The plane opens up with its machine guns strafing us as it passes overhead, so low I think, "I could have reached up and touched it." All of us troops watch as the plane passes to our rear and makes a wide "U" turn, flies a great distance to our front, make another wide turn and comes back at us with it's guns blazing.

During basic training we spend hours shooting at drones pulled in back of a small single engine airplane. The drone is connected to the plane by a very long rope so there is no danger of our live ammunition hitting the tow plane. When we are done with this exercise the plane and drone are landed and we inspect the drone for bullet holes and find very few, if any.

On this pass we are ready and waiting for the plane, so as soon as its guns fire and the bullets hit we all jump up and fire our rifles at the plane. I tell you here and now, "We would have done better by tossing our rifles into the air in front of the plane." The plane continues to travel on its course so it is soon out of our sight and never returns. Casualties suffered in this strafing stands at one; somehow when making my first dive behind the boulder, I scrapped it with my right hand and I am bleeding between my thumb and forefinger. I think, "I should report my slightly bloody hand to the medic, get a Purple Heart medal and go home, a hero," but I just pass it off. Had the plane's pilot caught us a few hundred yards back or forward of our position with no boulders for cover there would have been carnage.

CHAPTER
32

THE MAJOR

Early morning finds my entire company assembled by the side of a highway that runs parallel to a river, flowing from our right to our left. Looking to our right we can see a city in the distance. Instructions from my company commander are: "Mister Lee, follow the highway until you come to a bridge, cross it into the city and see what we are to encounter then report back to me."

Moving on point about three hundred yards out in front of Lt. Evans, with the rest of the troops following a short distance to his rear, I am abreast of the beginning buildings of the city. As I walk through a nice green meadow there is the asphalt highway on my left that is elevated about two feet above the level of the field. On the other side of the highway to my immediate left, there is a narrow strip of grass, then the river between me and the city. Row houses stand atop, and at the very edge of vertical river retaining wall, with the only break between the buildings being the opening for the town side of the bridge, about three hundred yards up ahead of me.

Approaching the lone bridge that spans the river, I experience an unusual happening; I get to read the cities sign, "CHAM." I am about to make my crossing of the bridge, when I look back and see Lt. Evans, motioning for me to come back to his position. When I get to him, he tells me, "The major called saying he wants to talk to you and that he will be here shortly, so just wait for him." After a period of time the major arrives, sitting in the back seat, on the passenger side of a jeep, with the only other person being the driver. The driver pulls over to the very edge of the right side of the pavement and stops on the highway parallel to where Lt. Evans and I are standing. Leaving the Lieutenant and approaching the jeep, I have my rifle slung on my right shoulder. Stopping next to the jeep, I am standing in the field so the major's eyes and my eyes are at about the same level, with a distance of about two feet separating us.

The major exclaims, "Mister Lee."

I reply, "Yes sir," We are not vain enough to exchange salutes.

He says, "I have reservations about you crossing that bridge, so wait until I set up some cover fire for you. Give me about twenty minutes to." There is a crack of a rifle from the city; the bullet hitting the major, in the back of his head, and zinging as it just misses my right ear, causing my face and upper field jacket to get spattered with blood and membrane.

Throwing all caution aside, I snatch my rifle from my shoulder and run towards the bridge, for although I was looking at the major as he spoke, I had been subconsciously looking past him, at the open window from where the sniper had fired the shot. In a fraction of a second I had counted the number of houses in the row to the open window to be six houses from the bridge, so crossing the bridge, I go to my left to the house, find the door open, and entering it I find no sniper, only the acrid smell of gun powder. The sniper had probably been stationed in the house to fire a shot, causing a delaying action on our part, giving the German troops a little more time to evacuate the city. He most likely had a vehicle waiting to make his hasty get away. As I have stated before, I have no desire to look for a shell casing as a souvenir. Returning back across the bridge, I report to Lt. Evans what I had found, and tell him, "All is clear to enter the city."

I had again probably been in the sights of an enemy rifle, as I traversed the entire length of the field, and been allowed to pass while the sniper waited for a bigger fish. I can not comprehend why he had not picked off Lt. Evans, for surely the sniper could see he was leading the troops. When the Lt. called me back he must have known the Lt. was of some importance. How could he have known a more prominent figure would appear? Whatever the answer, his patience paid off for he got himself a whale. He probably never knew what a momentous achievement he had accomplished.

I do not know how the major knew I carried the moniker of, "Mister Lee," for this is the first time we ever met. I had no idea Mister Lee was used by others than my immediate associates, so I guess you could say this is quit a tribute, for a private to be addressed as, "Mister," by the upper echelon. My company crosses the bridge, moves through Cham without meeting anymore resistance, and we move on.

CHAPTER
33

FULDA

The direction of our advance makes us believe we are marching straight into Berlin, but these thoughts change when my platoon is transported by truck, to another area where we are ordered to move into the already cleared city of Fulda. The day is a sunny, bright, clear, Easter Sunday morning, as we dismount from the truck, and start our trek towards the city. As we are about to pass the entrance to a small valley, located to our left of the highway, a group of wonderful German women and children emerge from their homes, located around the valley entrance. I have no idea how these folks knew a large contingent of, (I do not know whether to say, enemy troops, or liberating troops,) would be passing by their community on this particular Easter morning? They are bearing tray after tray, laden with shelled, hard boiled eggs, and slices of plum cake, and they are in a jubilant, festive mood as they pass these out to the troops. I say without fear of contradiction, "this amount of food had to have been prepared in advance of our arrival."

With the German government taking most of the food from the people, I do not know why, or how these women have come up with all these goodies? This display of hospitality, gaiety and joy, shows, in reality, just who the German populace had to fear.

We are forbidden to accept hand outs from the populace because of the risk of intentional poisoning, but how can soldiers who have not had a decent meal in month, refuse such succulent offerings?

As the city comes into sight Lt. Evans relieves me and is acting in my capacity at point, advancing down the middle of the highway, for we are to walk right into town without encountering any resistance. Since Lt. Evans is performing my job, I again have time to think about how I had deprived some troops a few peach slices, and compare that to what a number of villagers must have sacrificed so us troops could enjoy Easter goodies.

To our left is a relatively deep ditch, and an embankment about five feet high, with a solitary house sitting back a few yards from its edge. After passing this house there is an open field several hundred yards long that extends from the ditch uphill until it reached the tree line. To our right the landscape tapers down until it reaches a river, then on the other side of the river the terrain rises up to another highway that is at about the same elevation as the one we are traversing.

Our six support tanks, that I had not seen since the bunker incident, are approaching the city via this highway on the other side of the river. The troops of my platoon and the tankers are waving to each other as we advance. Lt. Evans has already passed the house, and I am moving along the edge of the paved highway next to the ditch that has a cement drainage culvert at this point. I am parallel to the house, with my head a little above the embankment, and about level with the base of the house when the thoughts going through my mind are shattered by this terrible crack above me, as the projectile passes so close above me I think my ear drums have burst and my head has exploded.

Before I can dive over the edge of the culvert into the ditch I hear this awful explosion coming from the house. One of the tank's gunners fired just the one round, with the tank's big gun." Someone to my rear yells, "Medic! There are troops in there." He and several men rush into the building, and when they emerge they give us the sad news that all three of my squad are dead. The body of the third member of our foursome of greenhorn replacements is laying in the house, so it shakes me up a little as I think: "Our first member got shot up while on patrol, the second member had to be taken out of action because of his battle fatigue, and the third has just been killed by friendly fire, leaving me the only one remaining." I say to myself, "I'm going to make it and survive because no God damn bullet is going to get me. The offerings of the villagers have much more significance than you might imagine, for they turned out to be the last meal of a number of my squad."

When contact is finally established with the tank commander, his excuse is, "I detected movement in the house and assumed it was German soldiers. Sorry about that." What they had seen was several members of my squad who had entered the house to make sure it was cleared. When the proper people are notified by our radio man about the dead and their location, the company commander and I have again changed places and I move towards the city.

Three rows of one story barrack type buildings sit to the right of the highway, with the rows extending away from the highway, so I can look between the rows. As I pass the last building on my right, the five foot bank on my left rises to about thirty feet, with the face of it being a slanted concrete retainer wall that extends for about a hundred feet with the base of the wall located at the very edge of the paved highway. Just as I am about to clear the last building my observation shows an open field extends town to the river, and some premonition has me go into a crouch and dash the length of the wall with my rifle across my body at the ready. I am approximately midway of the wall when I hear several cracks of a rifle from down by the river and cement chips fly from the wall to my left. I make it to cover of the first building on my right at the end of the field without getting hit. One at a time each man from my platoon in turn crouches and runs past the wall, with a shot and chips, each time. Peering around the corner of the first building I attempt to locate the gunners position but have no luck. The distance is so great that by the time the gunmen sees an individual and fires, his shot is late and just pock marks the wall. When the last man, who is Lt. Evans has finished his run I think, "It is a miracle no one got hit."

At the end of the wall there is a cement stairway that we ascend to the top of the wall and occupy the large house sitting back a bit from the edge of the wall. Lt. Evans has guards man the windows, while the rest of the troops take a much needed breather. Two of us are standing at an open window looking down on the highway and can follow it along as it passes through the town, with the steep hill on the left, and buildings on the right. There is a large cave entrance at the base of the hill directly across the street from one of the buildings and as we watch a German soldier appears from one of the buildings and just saunters across the street towards the cave. He is in the center of the street when the two of us standing at the window simultaneously fire a shot from our rifles, the impact of the shells hitting him causes him to emit a terrible ear piercing death scream.

If you have never experienced the sound of the death scream I cannot describe it to you, but I will say, "It is such a high pitched, shrill scream, that it shatters your nerves to the point, you feel like screaming." This is the third time I have heard it.

We raise a few domestic rabbits down in our yard and I am the family butcher. Dad shows me how to kill a rabbit by holding it up by it's ears in my left hand and giving it a good hard karate-chop to the back of it's neck. I am following this procedure, but I do not hit it just right and my nerves are shattered as it emits this ear piercing scream so I give it another chop.

As I am walking down Ash Road approaching the junction with Fairfield Avenue, my uncle's horse drawn beer wagon is passing through the cobble stone junction when the horse slips and falls forward. I am close enough to hear the loud crack of its neck as it lands with its head twisted under its chest and it omits the death scream. The horse is not dead, so my uncle barrows a rifle from one of the nearby neighbors and puts the horse out of its misery.

We do not get any deeper into Fulda because late in the afternoon a truck arrives and transports us to another location, leaving the body of the German soldier still lying in the street. At the conclusion of our truck ride, back out on point in front of the troops, I have time to think and my conscious is beginning to bother me with this terrible thought. "In Germany, almost all working individuals wear some type of uniform that depicts the type of work they perform. Because of the great distance between the person we shot in the street in Fulda, it is possible we could have mistaken the uniform to be that of a soldier and we had killed a poor innocent civilian?" I do know one thing for certain; I have broken my ethic code of, "I will never kill an unarmed man." I can live with the thought that I have killed in self defense, but the doubt in my mind I have killed senselessly is a thought that is just too much to bear and I cannot clear this thought from my mind.

CHAPTER
34

SONNENBURG

The German army is in disarray and retreating fast, so my platoon receives orders to just walk right into the city of Sonnenburg, Germany. Early Sunday morning, the sun is shinning bright and the birds are chirping, so it is an unusually beautiful day as we approach the city.

I am on point walking down the middle of the highway, taking in the scenery, as if I am a tourist. The right side of the highway consists of fields about level with the road surface and is of no significance to me. The terrain to my left is almost a clone to the Fulda approach. The ditch to my left, right next to the asphalt, is enormously wide and deep, and the field has a gentle rise until meeting the tree line of the hill. A lone house to my left stands in the field about twenty feet back from the ditch, almost level with the road, then the field extends perhaps a distance of a hundred and fifty yards along the highway to the first row of houses of the city. Passing this house, I am perhaps fifty feet from where the highway enters the city, and to my right are rows of what look to be military barracks.

As I walk, I have my rifle across the front of my body at hip level with my left hand cradling the barrel and my right hand griping the trigger mechanism. As I pass the last row of these buildings I glance to my right and see an individual, I believe to be a German soldier, make a dash from a building towards what appears to be a small guard shack. By the time I swing my rifle around and fire a shot at him he is gone.

This act of firing my rifle is, I believe, the most stupid thing, and the most brilliant thing I have done since entering combat, for it most likely prevents the death of an untold number of troops. Once again I am in hell, because from the tree line at the upper end of the field to my left a machine gun opens up on me, and it seems either the gun is inaccurate or the gunner is inexperienced, because with the sound of the bullets passing around me, I whirl around, see the firing is coming from the tree line of the field, and I make my dive into the ditch without a single bullet hitting me.

Finding the ditch to be at least three feet deep, I attempt to stay out of the trickle of water flowing at the ditche's bottom and laying prone, I ponder, "What to do?" Lt. Evans and the troops close behind are about to pass the house when all this occurs. Nothing further happens for a while, so maintaining the effort to stay dry, crawling on my hands and knees I make my way back towards the house.

Encountering no one, I leave the ditch and move to the house. Entering, I fantasize being told something of this order, "It is a good thing you fired that shot, or we could have all moved up to that location and suffered a lot of casualties. We knew you were a goner! How the hell did you not get hit?"

In reality, this is what I hear from Lt. Evans, "Mister Lee, you got us into this, now get us out of it."

Looking the situation over I see nothing but the clear field space up to the tree line as well as to the row houses of the town. Re-entering the ditch I once again do my best to stay out of the water as I crawl to the edge of town. There I am facing the opening of a very large pipe that feeds the ditch. I contemplate crawling through this pipe and exiting it somewhere in the city, but as I peer into it I can see no light, so I scamper out of the ditch and dash along the highway, past the first building into the city.

There is one house, then a street leading up towards the woods on my left, so I turn left and proceed along this street until I came to the last house close to the woods. As I peer around its corner back towards the field I see a slightly level spot below the tree line, where the machine gunner is still laying behind the machine gun with his buddy laying just to his right. They had probably been posted there to fire one burst, causing us to delay our advance to give the troops more time to withdraw from the city. Then they are to make a hasty retreat. Things were so easy they probably decided to wait and give another burst from their gun. What a terrible mistake they had made. I look the edge of the woods over, I see no movements, but I can not take a chance there may be backups in the trees.

After my observation I stand my rifle against the building, remove a grenade from my left bandoleer with my right hand, pull the pin, release the lever, count to three, step out, toss the grenade in a underhand motion and the timing and throw are perfect. The grenade lands right between the gunner's head and the gun butt, exploding on contact with the ground, flipping the gun and raising the gunner and his buddy's head and torso into the air. I step back behind the house and peer around the corner, see no movement and cannot take the chance to go into the field to see if the soldiers are dead. I grab my rifle and make a beeline back down to the highway.

I have no communication with the troops in the house at this point in time, so I tie the white handkerchief on the end of my rifle barrel and signal the troops in. I signal and I wait, I signal and I wait, etc. and as time passes and seeing no movement I have the feeling I am an idiot, and have been abandoned once again. Time passes, so I move to the edge of the highway and sit on the bank and try to make some sense of what is going on. Removing my back pack, I recline on the bank trying to relax while I decide what action to take. Being exhausted I doze off and am awakened by the sound of a vehicle approaching from the direction of the house where the troops are supposed to be. It is a duce and a half and as it gets closer I get up and don my back pack, and move across the highway and await its arrival. Getting along side of me it stops and Lt. Evans is sitting in the passengers seat in the cab, and the whole first platoon in riding in back.

I ask, "What's going on,"

Without any explanation Lt Evans order, "Get out on point and move through town."

I decide right then and there, I will have my say.

"What happened, don't you give a shit whether I am alive or dead?"

"I said get out on point."

"I heard you but I'm not done making my report. Who's stupid idea was it to load a truck with troops and move across the face of a field that might have a machine gun covering it. If it is still there do you know what carnage it could cause."

"Enough! I said move out!"

"Okay, okay, but first I'll finish my report. The gun with two Kraut manning it, was still in place and I knocked them out with a grenade. Surely you must have heard the explosion?" It could have been me getting killed."

"Are you finished?"

"Yes, Sir."

"Alright I'll report it to headquarters." He orders me, "Now get moving on point, and move through town."

"I'm going! I'm going! But what the hell is going on? Aren't you going to give me some reason why you abandoned me?"

I receive no answer as to this strange happening, take up my position at point, and as I walk on the highway through town encountering no enemy troops, I am once again pissed off to the point I have a throbbing in my head. Walking with anger in my step, the distance between the truck and me increases to a much greater length than usual. I again do some thinking in the form of a question, "What the hell could have transpired in such a short time that would cause me to be abandoned." About to leave the city, all this is wiped out of my mind when I come to a compound on my right, with a very high chain link fence and a padlocked gate. Inside the compound a throng of women are pressing against the fence and the gate. Using my rifle butt to smash the padlock, I jump back as the gate swing open and the women overwhelm me with hugs and kisses, in their elation at being freed.

The truck carrying the troops shows up at this time, diverting the women's attention away from me, so I manage to free myself from the throng of poor, pathetic, awful smelling females. (I probably don't smell any better for the lack of bathing for so long.) It is astonishing how the women engulf and swarm over the truck and it's occupants. While the troops are entrapped by this masse, I enter the compound and find conditions almost too horrible to believe, with dead bodies lying here and there, I do not locate any water for washing and bathing, nor do I see any toilet facilities. I do not know how the women managed to survive. Leaving the compound with the freed prisoners still fussing with the troops, I get through the mass and move on, out of the city. Out on the open highway, the truck catches up to me. I climb aboard and we are taken to another area.

At this point I want to interject a thought. "Have you noticed how each time I am shot at by the enemy, the gunners aim is off, the gunners timing is off, the gun's accuracy is to be questioned, or I must have an invisible shield surrounding me?"

I ask the soldier sitting next to me, "What the hell happened?"

"Just as you got into town, Lt. Evans had us leave the house and retrace our route back along the highway, where we met up with the truck and we all climbed aboard." He tells me.

I respond with, "None of this makes any sense to me. Where is the logic to it all? What if I had not taken out the gunners, and they were still there? As the truck came past the field, one good burst from the machine gun could have wiped out the whole God-damn bunch of you."

The other troops hearing this statement exclaim, "Yea, we never thought about that ,but you're right. We all could have gotten killed."

CHAPTER
35

THE DAY PRESIDENT ROOSEVELT DIES

After walking the entire day without encountering any of the enemy, my platoon passes a farmhouse and approaches a tree lined dirt road running crosswise to our front. We are still in the farm yard and since darkness is setting in we call it a day. Lt. Evans has us spread out in the field just shy of the tree line, the best we can for the night. All night long we walk, we sit, we lay down, we do anything to beat the cold and we listen. The sounds we hear from the other side of the road are voices speaking in excited German, with an occasional shout. Evidently there are German troops directly across the road from us and besides the excited voices, we hear engines revving as they are probably loading vehicles getting ready to pull out.

They are just beyond the tree line on the other side of the road, so close, I think, "I can pelt them with stones if I had any." At first light we have heard no activity or voices from across the road for several hours, so Lt. Evans has me check it out. Crossing over the dirt road I see the foliage is all beat down and there is no sign of any enemy troops so I make my return back across the road and report, "The Krauts have pulled out."

Lt. Evans acknowledges my report, and with a raised voice shouts, "We will stay here until I get further orders, so let's go into the farmhouse and find out if they have anything we can eat. The Platoon has been depleted in number and we have had no replacements since my buddies and I had joined the outfit, so we all move into the house and find there is room for all. The only occupants are the farmer and his Frau.

When asked if they have any eggs, the Frau says in English, "Yes, but they belong to the government and if you eat them, we will be in trouble? The government keeps an accurate account of all our live stock and vegetables we produce. We have to keep tract of what we consume, because if the authorities think they are being shorted, we are punished severely."

We assure them, "The war is about over so you have nothing to fear from the soldiers, nor the officials. They will not be back." The Frau shows us several large baskets of eggs they have accumulated and we take what we can eat back to the kitchen. While she is scrambling a batch of these eggs in a large pot, I go out and catch a chicken, butcher it by holding its legs and wings firmly in my left hand, placing my forefinger and the index finger of my right hand behind its ears. Giving a quick twist and jerk, I pop the head off and instead of plucking the feathers; I use my hunting knife to dress and skin the carcass.

Someone finds a small radio the farmer has hidden, and as I am about to place the chicken into a pot of boiling water, he turns it on and we hear the words,

"President Roosevelt has died and Harry S. Truman is now president." We exclaim almost in unison, "Who the hell is Harry S. Truman?" The majority of us are men, too young to vote, so we are ignorant of our government politicians except for the president.

CHAPTER
36

THE DAY THE WAR ENDS

From the day we received word of the change in our countries presidency the days are uneventful until mid afternoon of 7 May, 1945, at approximately 1600 hours. My platoon is passing through a small town in Czechoslovakia when Lieutenant Evans receives word over the field phone, "The war is over." When he passes the word to us troops, we all shout with joy. His next words are, "The first thing everyone does, is go into a building and strip your weapons and give them a good cleaning."

My squad enters a building on our right, where everyone sits on the living room floor and disassembles his weapon. We no more than get them apart, when Llieutenant Evans comes in and says, "I just received the order to cross the Vlatava river up ahead, and occupy the town on the other side. Mister Lee, move out."

I tell him, "We need some time to reassemble our weapons."

"We have no time. Move out! Have you already forgotten the fighting is over? You don't need a weapon."

We all stuff our pockets with small parts, and jam the larger ones into the front of our jackets. I feel like a complete idiot moving out on point, with the barrel of my rifle stuck down inside the left of my jacket and the stock stuck in the right side. It is just a short distance to the river and as I approach the bridge. In my stride I have my right foot raised to step onto it when there is a sequence of explosions and I pull my foot back.

I can not see what the explosions are but the bridge settles right down into the river and sections are completely covered by water. This cut off any means of crossing the river, so we return to the small town and bed down in the buildings. This day, 7 May, 1945, I am seven weeks and five days shy of my nineteenth birthday.

POST WAR-WAR
CONNECTORS

Leukemia

This affliction takes place in late 1929 and over sixty years later, in 1991, I am being checked out for an aneurism in the inside of my left thigh and during testing I am once again diagnosed with Leukemia in my left femur. The Doctor recommends my femur be X-rayed every six month. After five years of X-rays it is determined that the spots in my bone marrow are spots from years past and they are dormant. I have now beaten leukemia twice.

First dead soldiers

The laughing by the battle hardened soldiers, to our reaction upon viewing the dead soldiers may have sounded cruel and ghoulish, showing disrespect for the dead, but they were not making fun of the dead, they were merely making jest of our greenhorn reactions. We later find the best way to deal with finding the man next to you laying there dead even though it is sad, and heart wrenching is to just take a big gulp of air and make light of the situation. If a soldier is to let the least bit of sentiment creep in, he will surely break down or go mad. Who knows, "You may be the next laugh."

Thanks to adversaries

This will offend multitudes of war veterans, but I have to tell it like it is, from my personal experiences, and way of thinking. The war in Europe is over and this may be a strange thing to say, but I feel I owe thanks to the German soldiers for my being alive today. Numerous times they had me in their sights, but refrained from firing. Once I had failed to draw fire, or detect their position and passed, our main force was vulnerable to their fire, costing the lives of so many good men. I now render a belated apology to the men I let down. "Thanks you for my life, German soldiers."

Guard duty

This is not a war story but something on the order of what Beetle Bailey of the comics would do. After the war ends, I am in route back to the States and spent several days in a processing camp in France. While there, I am assigned to guard duty. As the rounds are made in the wee hours of the night posting the new sentries and relieving the old ones I am put on post number one.

The weather is cold and it is raining so after just a few minutes at my post, I think, "After all the hardship and misery I have been through I am an idiot for putting up with this," so I leave my post, return to the guard house and go back to bed. When morning comes, the sergeant of the guard assembles us to relieve us of guard duty and, announces, "Last night someone cheated because when I returned the guard detail to the guard house, there were not enough bunks for everyone." Can you believe I got away with something so stupid?

Hot toddy and Easter treats

We are all familiar with the quote, "War is hell." It is my humble opinion this quote should state, "War is mostly hell." I make this statement because the event by the stocks was just the first of several times the populace of various communities show their gratitude to me and the others. This also proves that something beautiful can be found in everything if you just learn how to look for it. All these years I have felt guilty for not being able to get in touch with that angel in Luxembourg, to thank her for being so very thoughtful and kind to me in making that hot toddy for me, and shivering with me as I drank it. I also feel down because I have not been able to thank the women of that hamlet located on the approach to Fulda. If by chance any of you beautiful people involved in these two incidents reads the above words, "I thank you from the bottom of my heart."

Bunker

By the time I joined my platoon after the bunker incident, the tanks and their crews were gone, because they did their thing, "pulling back to a safe location to spend the night," for they are very vulnerable in the darkness. I related to everyone what had transpired, but the tanks never came back after that, so I imagine to this day the tankers believe they silenced that machine gun.

The Major

EULOGY TO MAJOR JOSEPH P. BOUCHER

As we approached the city of Cham, Germany, in mid morning, of April 25, 1945, Major Joseph P. Boucher, knowing the war is winding down could have used his high stature in the army to remain at the rear echelon, where he could have sat out the remainder of the war in relative safety, assuring his returning home to his loved ones a whole healthy person.

Instead, on this morning, unknowingly just twelve days before the war ends in Europe, he chose to come forward to the front lines on the outskirts of Cham, Germany for the sole purpose of making an effort to keep me, a lowly private first class, from walking into unknown enemy armament on the far side of the bridge, as I was about to make a solitary crossing into the city.

Major Boucher and I were looking directly into each other's eyes when that fatal shot rang out. I feel the major went beyond the call of duty by showing his greatness as a leader who had so much compassion, for his troops that he would give up his life for all his subordinates, regardless of their lowly rank.

PS:
    Major Boucher's attempts to protect me were unnecessary, as I found out when I made my run across

the bridge in pursuit of the sniper, encountering no resistance. I hope Mmajor Boucher was personally given God's blessings upon his arrival and I say, "May God have blessed the Major."

Souvenirs

MY HUNTING KNIFE

You say, "The hunting knife you carried and used during your days in combat has a story behind it so surely you saved it as a souvenir." That I did, but a strange occurrence or incident happened.

In 1948 I am attached to the Navy's Submarine Mine Depot and stationed at Fort Monroe, Virginia. I am 100 % Army and I am single, so all my worldly possessions are in my foot locker, in my upright cloth locker and of course my shoes and boots are under my metal framed cot. I take a thirty day leave and when I return to camp to sign in, I find the building I was billeted in is vacated and all closed up.

Reporting to post headquarters I am informed, "The Submarine Mine Depot has been completely disbanded." Headquarters does not have any record of me and does not know what to do with me, so they put me up in the fort guest house until they can get the pentagon to issue me a new assignment.

Efforts to locate my belongings and gear I had left in the barracks are futile, so I lost everything but the clothes on my back and the ones I took on leave. I had to be issued everything all over again. I often wonder what the consequences would have been had I just turned and walked away from the Army?

My cherished knife was locked in my foot locker, so I lost a dear friend.

Atrocities

There are three incidents I have written about that leave me confused.

1. I have contacted The British embassy in the United States about the freeing of the British airmen and the embassy has no interest.

2. I have contacted a number of organizations that catalogue the holocaust about the people in the, "field of horror," and no one is interested.

3. I have not been able to locate any spoken of, or written word, about the prison camp located in the outskirts of Sonnenburg, Germany.

Innuendos and Implications

I have made several references to what is termed atrocities and just plain murder by the troops of my company, yours truly included. War does strange things to a person's mind. Until you have experienced and endured the bitter cold, the hunger, the ever present thought and action of kill or be killed, day after day, week after week that eventually turns into month after month as the battle hardened troops that participated in the, "Battle of the

Bulge," from beginning to end went through, do not make judgment.

Being a combatant for just a short period of the winding down of the Battle of the Bulge, I found it hard to imagine my enduring the misery and extremely harsh conditions these courageous soldiers endured and persevered until they were victors. I personally do not believe I was man enough to have endured what these soldiers went through? One has to wonder as to why they did not all go insane?

Epilogue to 28 prisoners

Upon publication of this book, anyone with good hearing had better insert ear plugs, for upon reading this article there will be a great scream emitted by all of New England's residents, plus all military officers and I will become an endangered species. Perhaps you, the reader, may even join in the utterance, for the words you are digesting will be a slap in the face to all the above mentioned personnel and my veracity will be put to its extreme test. This happening is so unethical that all will deny it could have taken place. It really hurts me to write this article but I reiterate, "Every word in this book is truth so it must contain the good as well as the bad." I am an old man and I stick by my conviction, "I will not humiliate any man," so I state no names and I feel I am still strong enough to weather the criticism so here goes.

Post war finds the 101st Regiment consolidated and garrisoned in and around the small community of Pilsen,

Czechoslovakia. My company commander summons me and informs me, "Papers have been submitted to get you a citation for the capture of those twenty eight Germans." I reply to the news with, "That's nice."

The lieutenant singles me out and tells me, the paper work came back and it has been approved for the Silver Star; the only problem is, your name has been replaced with another man's name, who is from the Boston area, the home center of the Division."

I exclaim, "But this man wasn't even along on the skirmish."

The Lt. says, "I know it, but don't worry because, it was just one award, and you have been put in for five more citations that are greater deeds than the capture."

When a regimental parade is set up to honor the Silver Star recipient, I am approached once again by my company commander, and I am told, "Mister Lee, I can't humiliate you any more than you have already been by having you pay homage to another man for your deed, so you are excused from the parade."

When the paper work for the other awards come back, my C. O. comes to me yet another time and informs me, "They have all been judged in the line of duty and I figure the only ones getting awards are the personnel from the New England area."

Silver Star

I want to stress the fact that in this writing, I am not trying to humiliate any man for something beyond his control, for I know how hard it would be to refuse to be a hero. One thing you will have to admit is certain, every military outfit needs heroes, so, there have been a few men and women who have had awards lavished on them without the individual ever making a claim of performing a heroic deed. When the fraudulent awards are exposed, the individual is reduced from a hero to a fraud, thus being humiliated through no fault of his own.

I will not divulge the name of this man who accepted the silver star, for I feel nothing but pity for the poor soul, who has lived a lie all these years. I would love to hear the narration he has given for this deed and medal. I ask any man or woman who condemns these short lived heroes to step forward with your stones; but do not wait for me to join you, for I will not be there. The Department of the Army, Military Awards Department, discovering a few of these fraudulent awards. have had them rescinded.

Revelations

After reading the book, History of the 26th Division's 50th Anniversary, I read it again three more times and discover there were many medals awarded to a spectrum of individuals from a conglomerate of states all across America. So, I had been duped. This time I had not been duped by the enemy but by the man I revered most in the world, "My company commander."

At the time of this happening I was still shy of my nineteenth birthday and never gave a thought to ask, "Let me see the paper work," for the 1ˢᵗ Lt.'s words were gospel to me. I now cannot make any sense of the situation that happened just after the end of WW11 that I am now discussing and I am one confused old man.

The words spoken to me by my company commander, were ether words of his own convictions, or, and this does not have any logic to it, he was just leading me on. If none of this were true, why would he single me out and spin such a yarn, when he could have just ignored the whole thing?

My Apologies

I make no excuses for the negative feelings I carried all these years, but I do ask all of the officers of the Yankee Division to picture my mind set at the time and to forgive me for being so gullible. I now want to extend my most, <u>Sincere, from the bottom of my heart apology</u> to you for believing any of you could be so unethical. One last word in closure; having said all the terrible things I have in this epilogue, I ask that I be taken back into the folds of the Yankee Division.

I am now proud that I was, and always will be a: "YANKEE."

EPILOGUE

All through the years, right up the turn of the century I have always maintained that my mind was too strong for me to be brainwashed. Upon joining The Yankee Division Veterans Association in the year 2000 and reading, The History of the 26th YANKEE DIVISION, I discover that my state of mind was just a fallacy. Please bear with me as I attempt to clarify my state of mind and thinking for all of these years.

Recall the words of my company commander about the awards; "The only problem is, your name has been replaced with another man's name, who is from the Boston area, the home center of the division," and his second utterance, "I figure the only ones getting awards are the personnel from the New England Area."

I have written how, "I could not develop and carry a hatred for any man," but hearing the above phrases gives me an acrid taste in my mouth and I come very close to hating the high command of the 26th Infantry Division for their being so unethical. I am ashamed to have been a part of the Division, so I never mentioned the division I served with in the Bulge to a living sole.

EPILOGUE

ABOUT THE AUTHOR

At the conclusion of WW11, Private First Class Irvin Lee Boring is discharged from the army and true to their word, Bethlehem Steel hires him back in his old job as a welder with the Bethlehem Steel Corporation. After two years of inhaling the welding smoke, the welding fumes, and seeing men die of suffocation because their lungs have filled to capacity with these toxins, he becomes disenchanted with his job, so he reenlist in the army. With a total of eight years of formal education, in eight years he attains the rank of first sergeant.

With twenty two years of service behind him and stuck in the jungles of Thailand well past his rotation date, he become disenchanted with the army and submits his retirement request. When the request arrives on the post commanders desk, first sergeant Boring is ordered to report to the camp commanders office. Standing before the colonels desk, he is informed, "The army needs you and nine month ago you signed papers stating you would reenlist, so if you follow through with this request I will have you court marshaled for breach of contract." He informs the colonel; "I have had it, so submit the papers."

While awaiting his retirement orders, first sergeant Boring receives orders to become sergeant major of Fort Knox, Kentucky; it is every sergeant's dream to achieve the prestigious position and rank of sergeant major." He would be sergeant major in name only, without the rank and pay of E9, because he has already been officially informed by the department of the army that because of his poor eye sight and hearing problem, he can never be promoted even if a waver is requested. He turns down the position and retires at the age of forty.

At age seventy nine the doctors tell him, "There is nothing more we can do to save your heart, you have only a few month to live. Your heart is dried up like a piece of shoe leather, it is skipping so many beats, all the chambers are out of sync and your heart is only seven percent efficient." The Doctors also inform him, "You are so weak and feeble you cannot live alone anymore." He is sent home with the promise, "We will keep you as pain free as possible until you expire."

At home; he buys miniature tools, sits on a bucket, and does yard landscaping work. It is hard, but he pushes himself to the limit, so his childhood habit of beating the odds and recovering from all his afflictions kicks in and his body develops muscles. In eighteen month his heart muscles once again become pliable, the skipping is practically eliminated, his heart is back in sync and it now ten percent efficient:

Now at the age of eighty three years of age his heart is up to thirty five percent and he is a bit of a celebrity, for all his doctors tell him, "We cannot understand it, because instead of your body going through the aging process, your records indicate you are becoming younger every day. This brings up another point he has written about, "At the age of eighteen he is a man without the years, now he has the years of an old man but not the mind and body to go with the age."

One last note about the author: In June of the year 2004, he is declared legally blind and cannot renew his drive's license. His Optometrist informs him, "I cannot correct your vision anymore than I already have; I suggest you think about having lens implants and there is no guarantee they will improve your vision."

The first lens is implanted in his left eye on July 27th, 2005 and immediately upon getting off of the operating table he reads the eye chart and the eye is 20/30. One week later he has the right eye done and it improves to 20/20. He considers this a miracle and wonders, "Had I this good vision sixty five years earlier, just what could I have been, and what could I have accomplished?"